W9-CBI-793

SCRAPBOOK

A LIFETIME OF MEMORIES • *by* DAVID FISCHER

RUNNING PRESS
PHILADELPHIA • LONDON

First published in the United States in 2008 by
Running Press Book Publishers

Printed in China

9 8 7 6 5 4 3 2 1
Digit on the right indicates the number of this printing

Library of Congress Control Number: 2007937893

ISBN-13: 978-0-7624-3322-3
ISBN-10: 0-7624-3322-1

Cover images: (baseball) Sotheby's; (tickets) National Baseball Hall of Fame Library, Cooperstown, NY; (stadium photo) Al Bello/Getty Images

Cover design: Todd Bates
Design: Kasey Free
Editorial: Meghan Cleary
Photo Research: Chris Campbell
Production Coordination: Shirley Woo

A Yankee Stadium Scrapbook: A Lifetime of Memories is produced by
becker&mayer!, Bellevue, Washington
www.beckermayer.com

This book may be ordered by mail from the publisher.
Please include $2.50 for postage and handling.
But try your bookstore first!

Running Press Book Publishers
2300 Chestnut Street
Philadelphia, PA 19103-4371

Visit us on the web!
www.runningpress.com

CONTENTS

Vintage postcards depicting Yankee Stadium

Introduction

As we look back at the history of Yankee Stadium and try to capture its many memorable moments and personalities in one volume, we've got good news and bad news. The good news is that so many legends have been created here, so many records smashed, so many unforgettable victories won that it's difficult to whittle it down to so few pages.

This ballpark holds what few—if any—in history do: the mark of greats like Ruth and Gehrig, Mantle and DiMaggio, Jackson and Jeter. And Ruffing, Ford, Guidry, Rivera, Huggins, McCarthy, and Torre. Even Martin and Lemon and Steinbrenner—Yankee Stadium is home to all these giants and more.

These walls have witnessed events that are carved indelibly into the collective memory of baseball, like Ruth's first homer in the brand-new stadium, Gehrig's farewell speech, DiMaggio's 56-game hitting streak, Maris's 61st, Reggie's three-for-three, Boggs's exultant horseback ride, Jeter's unforgettable dive . . .

All the sights and sounds of the ballpark are here, too. Those famous blue seats, those high, scalloped edges, those soaring decks, so unlike anything that had come before (and few that have come since). The Big Bat! Monument Park, with plaques and memorials to all those ghosts and more. The Boss's box. "River Ave. and 161st St., next stop, Yankee Stadium!" Climbing down from the No. 4 train with thousands of other anxious fans.

The view, as you come out of a tunnel and see that Central Park of outfield grass, those clean blue walls, the peek of skyline above the outfield fences. A day game under a high, Yankee-blue sky . . . a night game with starlight dimmed by the shining Stadium. The clatter of the subway above the muted hum of the pregame crowd. "God Bless America" in the seventh. The softly sonorous, oh-so-familiar voice of Bob Sheppard—"Now batting for the Yankees . . . number 2 . . . Derek Jeter . . . shortstop . . . number 2." All that, my friends, is more than you could fit in a hundred scrapbooks.

You'll relive your own memories as you page through these—your first game with your dad, your kids' first Yankee hot dog, the time you got Jeter's autograph, that day you saw a Red Sox fan cry, all those wonderful days and nights in the most famous, most beautiful, most stirring baseball palace in the country.

Of course you know the bad news is that they're tearing down our beloved Yankee Stadium—but they're building a brand-new one. So as we close the book on the current stadium, you can hold your breath for the coming era of a whole new recordbook-full of new stories to tell.

INNING

1

the 1920s

The cranes swing up the steel and the Babe swings the lumber: Yankee Stadium opens in 1923 and instantly becomes America's baseball showplace. Ruth rewrites the home run record books (hitting more in this decade than any other player had in a career!). Ruth and Gehrig head up Murderer's Row as New York crowns its new home with three World Series titles in the decade.

"I want the greatest ballpark in the world."

—COLONEL JACOB RUPPERT, owner of the New York Yankees

Yankee Stadium in 1925

ABOVE The original home of the Yankees was Hilltop Park, a small wooden ballpark in Manhattan, at one of the highest spots in New York City, and so the club was known as the New York Highlanders. In 1913, the Highlanders changed their name to the Yankees and moved into the Polo Grounds, also home to their National League rivals, the Giants.

RIGHT This player transfer document paved the way for Harry Frazee, Boston Red Sox owner, to sell Babe Ruth to the Yankees for $125,000 in January 1920 and change the course of history for both teams. The player they would call "the Sultan of Swat" drew so many fans to the Polo Grounds, that the Yankees began outdrawing the Giants, souring the relationship between the two teams. In 1921, the Giants told the Yankees to make plans to leave the Polo Grounds.

UNIFORM AGREEMENT

FOR TRANSFER OF A PLAYER

NOTICE.—To establish uniformity in action by clubs when a player, released by a major league club to a minor league club, or by a minor league club to a major league club, refuses to report to and contract with the club to which he is transferred, the Commission directs the club securing him to protect both parties to the deal from responsibility for his salary during his insubordination by promptly suspending him.
Payment, in part or in whole, of the consideration for the release of such player will not be enforced until he is reinstated and actually enters the service of the purchasing club.

TO OR BY A

Major League Club

WARNING TO CLUBS.—Many contentions that arise over the transfer of players are directly due to the neglect of one or both parties to promptly execute and file the Agreement. The Commission will no longer countenance dilatory tactics, that result in appeals to it to investigate and enforce claims which, if made a matter of record, as required by the laws of Organized Base Ball, would not require adjustment. In all cases of this character, the complaining club must establish that it is not at fault for delay or neglect to sign and file the Agreement upon which its claim is predicated. (See last sentence of Rule 10.)

This Agreement, made and entered into this 26th day of December 1919

by and between Boston American League Baseball Club
(Party of the First Part)

and American League Base Ball Club of New York
(Party of the Second Part)

Witnesseth: The party of the first part does hereby release to the party of the second part the services of Player George H. Ruth under the following conditions:

(Here recite fully and clearly every condition of deal, including date of delivery; if for a money consideration, designate time and method of payment; if an exchange of players, name each; if option to recall is retained or privilege of choosing one or more players in lieu of one released is retained, specify all terms. No transfer will be held valid unless the consideration, receipt of which is acknowledged therein, passes at time of execution of Agreement.)

By herewith assigning to the party of the second part the contract of said player George H. Ruth for the seasons of 1919, 1920 and 1921, in consideration of the sum of Twenty-five Thousand ($25,000.) Dollars cash and other good and valuable considerations paid by the party of the second part, receipt whereof is hereby acknowledged.

The parties to this Agreement further covenant to abide by all provisions of the National Agreement and by all Rules of the National Commission, regulating the transfer of the services of a player, particularly those printed on the reverse side of this Agreement.

In Testimony Whereof, we have subscribed hereto, through our respective presidents or authorized agents, on the date above written:

SEAL

Witness:

BOSTON AMERICAN LEAGUE BASEBALL CLUB
(Party of the First Part) President

AMERICAN LEAGUE BASE BALL CLUB OF NEW YORK
Jacob Ruppert Prst
(Party of the Second Part)

Corporate name of Company, Club or Association of each party should be written in first paragraph and subscribed hereto. (See Rule 10.)

Club officials are cautioned to carefully read the provisions of the National Agreement and the rules of the National Commission, printed on the back of this Agreement, for their information and guidance.

LEFT The Yankees purchased a ramshackle ten-acre property at 161st Street and River Avenue from the estate of William Waldorf Astor for $675,000 on February 6, 1921. The property's location in the Bronx, ironically, is directly across the Harlem River from the Polo Grounds in Manhattan. The White Construction Company of New York broke ground on the site on May 5, 1922. It would take only 284 days to complete the project at a cost of just $2.5 million. This early construction shot taken on August 23, 1922 shows the steel framework beginning to take shape. The undertaking eventually involved 2,200 tons of structural steel and more than one million brass screws.

BELOW A postcard sold at Yankee Stadium in 1923 shows the original 1921 architect's model, in which Yankee Stadium's third deck was designed to be fully enclosed. But that idea was scaled back and the upper grandstands were never completed for the outfield sections.

"If they move to the Bronx, they may never be heard from again." —JOHN MCGRAW, Giants manager

April 18, 1923. On the day Yankee Stadium opened, 74,217 fans packed themselves inside. Before the game, Ruth had told a reporter, "I'd give a year of my life if I can hit a home run in this first game in this new park."

"Governors, generals, colonels, politicians, and baseball officials gathered together solemnly today to dedicate the biggest stadium in baseball, but it was a ball player who did the real dedicating. In the third inning, with two teammates on the base lines, Babe Ruth smashed a savage home run into the right-field bleachers, and that was the real baptism of the new Yankee Stadium. That also won the game for the Yankees, and all the ceremony which had gone before was only a trifling preliminary." —THE NEW YORK TIMES, April 18, 1923

LEFT In pregame festivities, John Phillip Sousa and the Seventh Regiment Band raise the Stars and Stripes along with the Yankees' 1922 pennant at the flagpole in deep center field.

BELOW The Yankees broke in the stadium with a 4-1 victory over the Boston Red Sox. The Bambino christened the place by hitting a three-run homer in the third inning off Howard Ehmke. From day one, "The House That Ruth Built" was an apt nickname, since it was Ruth that hit the first home run in the Stadium. Bob Shawkey was the Yankees' winning pitcher.

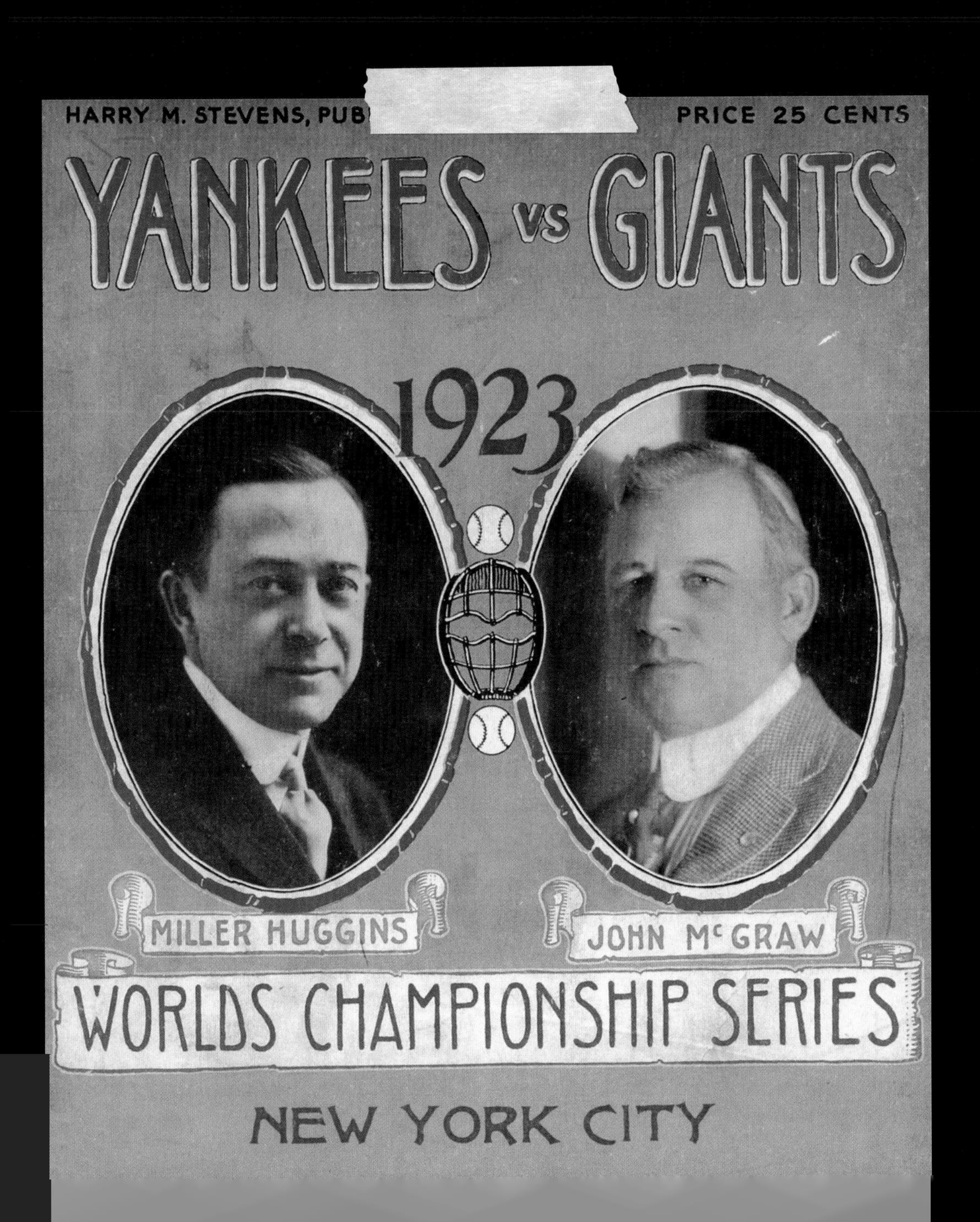

OPPOSITE President Warren G. Harding congratulates Babe Ruth after one of Ruth's home runs during the April 24, 1923, game against the Washington Senators. The 4-0 Yankee victory that day was the first shutout in the new stadium. (What would become the most recognizable insignia in sports—the interlocking NY monogram—did not appear on the Yankees' jerseys until 1936.)

LEFT The Yankees' manager Miller Huggins opened the new stadium to great fanfare by defeating John McGraw's Giants in six games to win the 1923 World Series, the first Subway Series. Ruth walloped three home runs and pitcher Herb Pennock won two games to help the team to the first of their twenty-six world championships.

"To understand him you had to understand this: He wasn't human." —JOE DUGAN, teammate

"No one hit home runs the way Babe did. They were something special, like homing pigeons. The ball would leave the bat, pause briefly, suddenly gain its bearings, then take off for the stands." —DIZZY DEAN, Hall of Fame pitcher for the St. Louis Cardinals

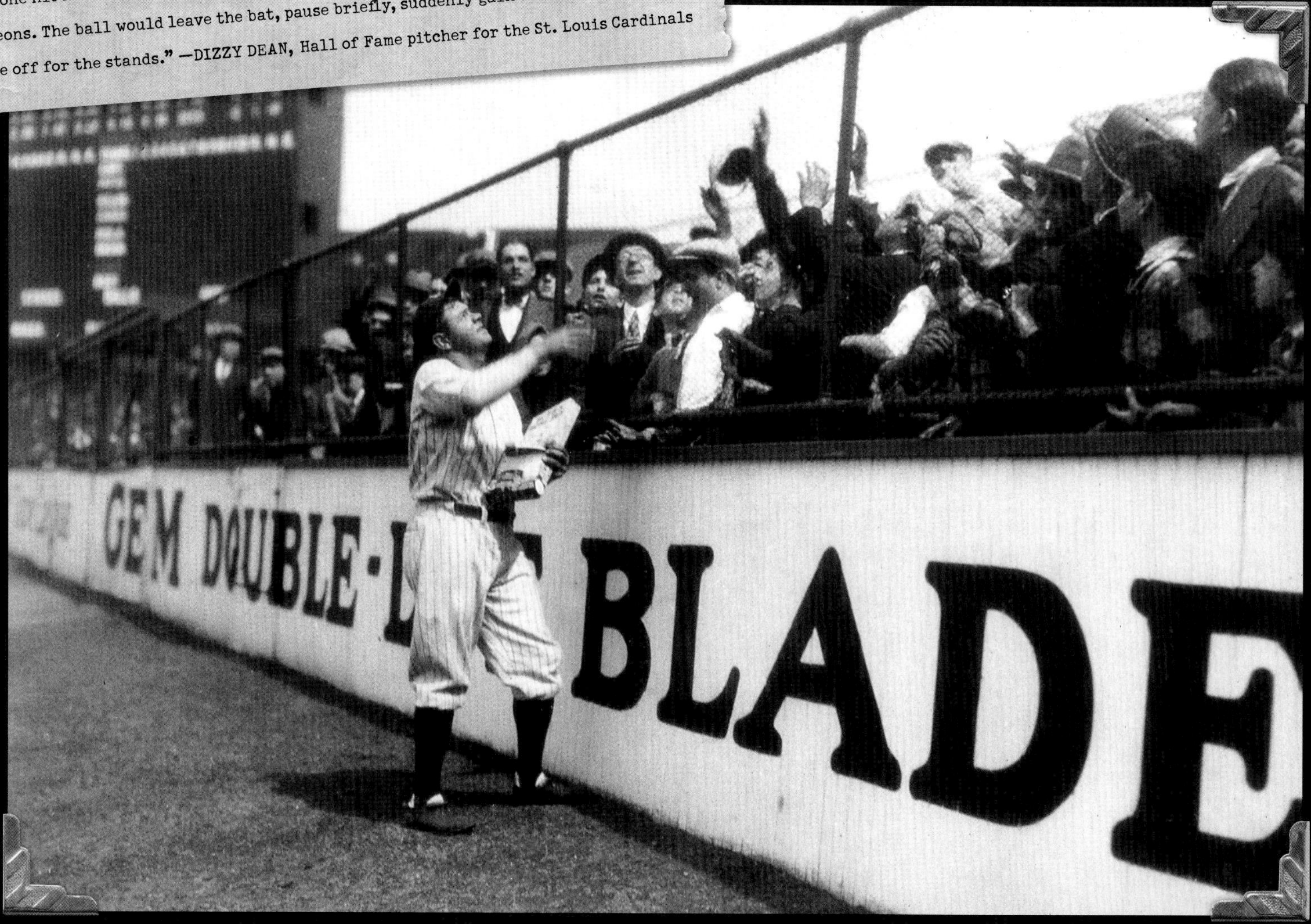

Sharing candy bars with fans in June 1928

ROLL OF HONOR
Babe Ruth

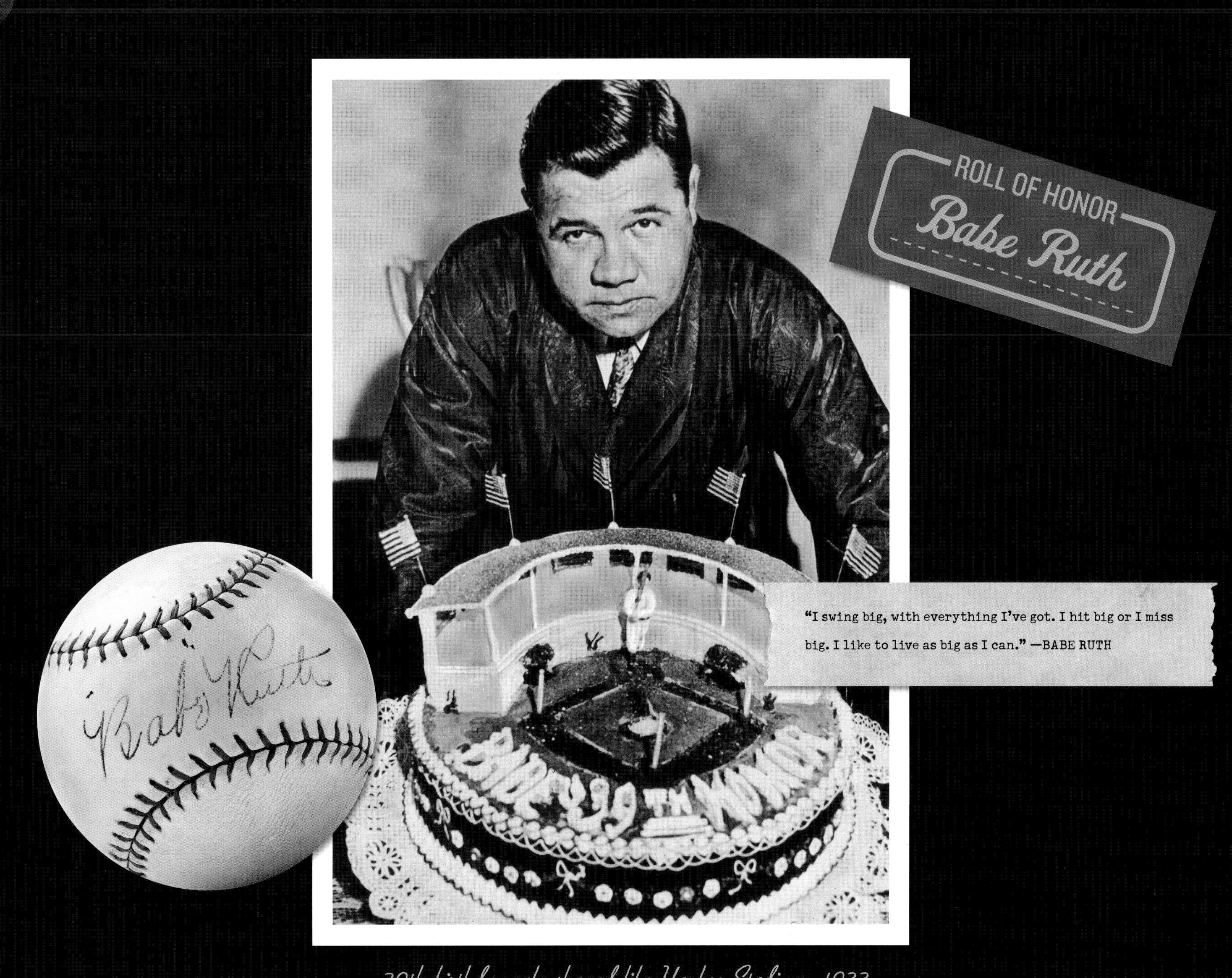

"I swing big, with everything I've got. I hit big or I miss big. I like to live as big as I can." —BABE RUTH

39th birthday cake shaped like Yankee Stadium, 1933

Babe Ruth hits his record-breaking 60th home run in the 1927 season off Tom Zachary of the Washington Senators at Yankee Stadium on September 30. When he went to right field in the top of the ninth, fans waved handkerchiefs and the Babe responded with military salutes. In the clubhouse after the game, Ruth boasted, "Let's see someone top that." Nobody took the invitation for thirty-four years. The 1927 Yankees, known as "Murderer's Row," won 110 games and lost only 44 for a .714 winning percentage. They took the pennant by nineteen games.

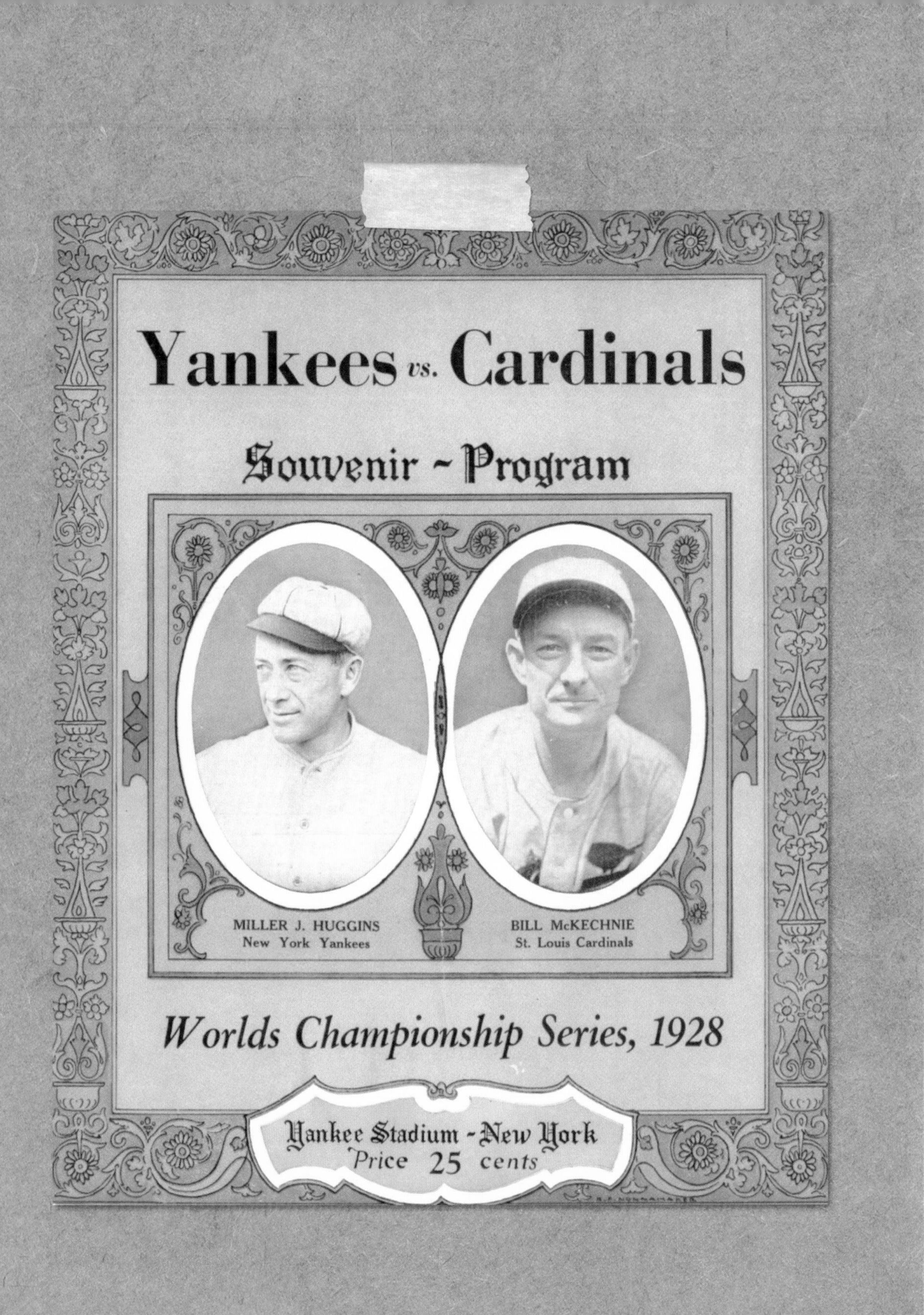

The Yankees beat the Cardinals in four straight games to win the 1928 title. It was the second straight Series sweep for manager Miller Huggins's team, considered by many to be one of the best teams ever.

With the addition of temporary seating, college football immediately found a home at Yankee Stadium with powerhouse Northeastern teams. West Virginia and Penn State, pictured here on October 27, 1923, played to a 13-13 tie six months after the gates opened.

Notre Dame football coach Knute Rockne delivered a fabled, emotional speech at Yankee Stadium on November 10, 1928. Faced with a scoreless tie at halftime against Army, Rockne urged his players to "win one for the Gipper," referring to George Gipp, an Irish player who had died of pneumonia eight years before. The inspired Fighting Irish went on to beat the Army Cadets, 12-6. Here Rockne (pictured far left) poses for a photo with Frank Carideo, Mayor James Walker, and his secretary ex-judge Andrews, as the mayor presents Carideo with a watch.

Ruth moves on . . . and Gehrig steps up. The Iron Horse appears in every game played at Yankee Stadium in the decade—until ALS finally stops him in 1939. The 1930s include five Yankees titles, including four in a row, but end with Gehrig's famous farewell speech. No, Lou . . . we were the lucky ones.

"The luckiest thing I ever did was sign with the Yankees. When you're with really great players, they pull you along." —RED ROLFE, third baseman

Aerial view of the Stadium in 1939

After a three-year absence, the World Series returned to the Bronx on a rainy Wednesday afternoon, September 28, 1932, but the inclement weather kept many away from the ballpark. A crowd of just 41,459 came out to watch the Yankees defeat the Chicago Cubs, 9-3, in the series opener.

LEFT Sports-radio announcer Ted Husing mans the microphone for CBS Radio to describe all the action of the 1932 Series. The Yankees defeated the Chicago Cubs in four straight games.

BELOW Joe DiMaggio makes his major league debut against the St. Louis Browns at Yankee Stadium on May 3, 1936. DiMaggio would begin wearing No. 5 the following season, when he led the league with a career-best 46 home runs.

1932 World Series ring

LEFT New York City mayor Fiorello LaGuardia watches the opening game of the 1937 World Series between the Yankees and the Giants from his box at Yankee Stadium. The Yankees beat their crosstown rivals in that Series for the second straight season.

BELOW Early "bleacher creatures," 1937. That year, the right-field grandstand was enlarged to three decks and extended to its current point, allowing upper-deck home runs to both fields.

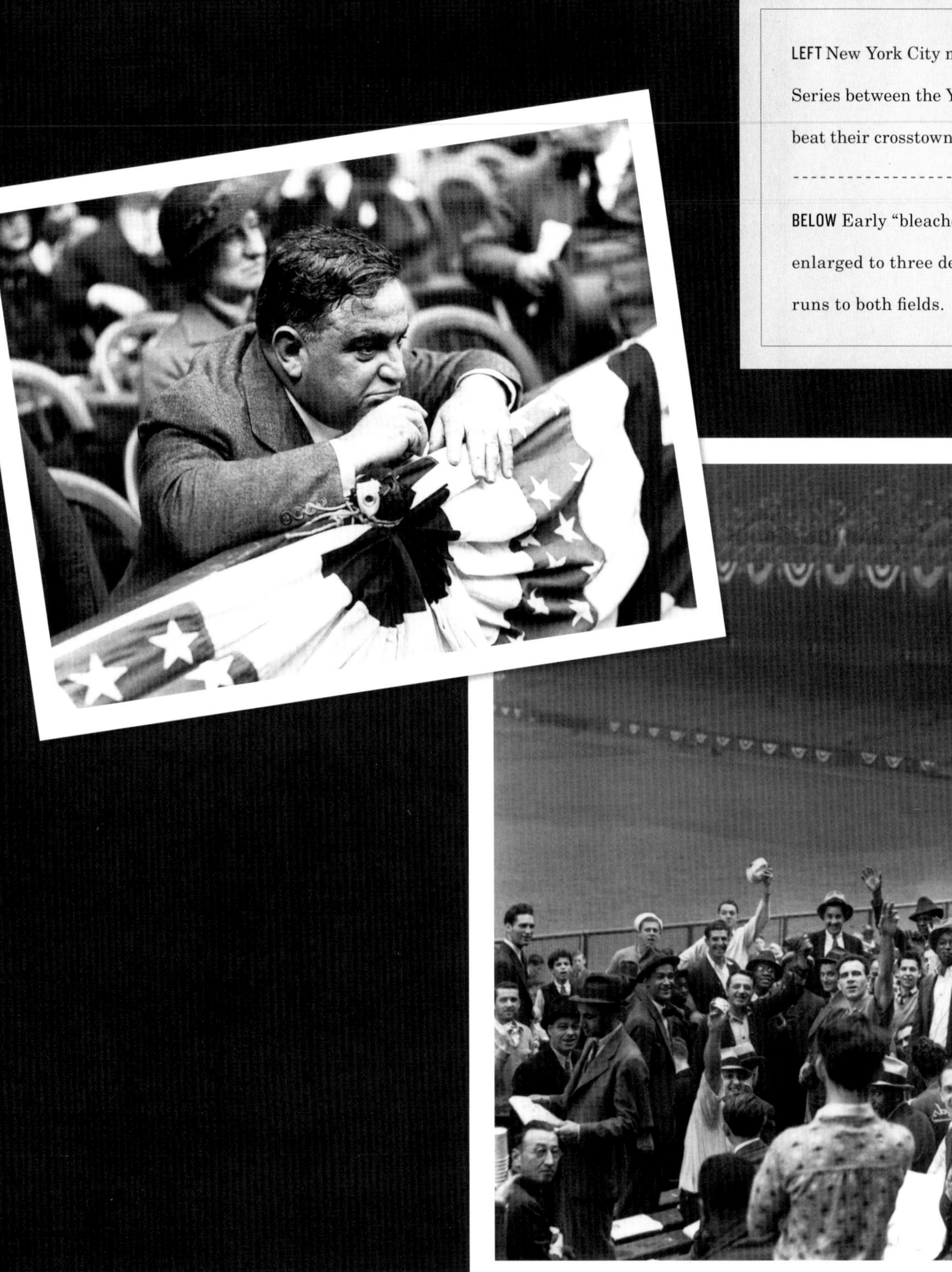

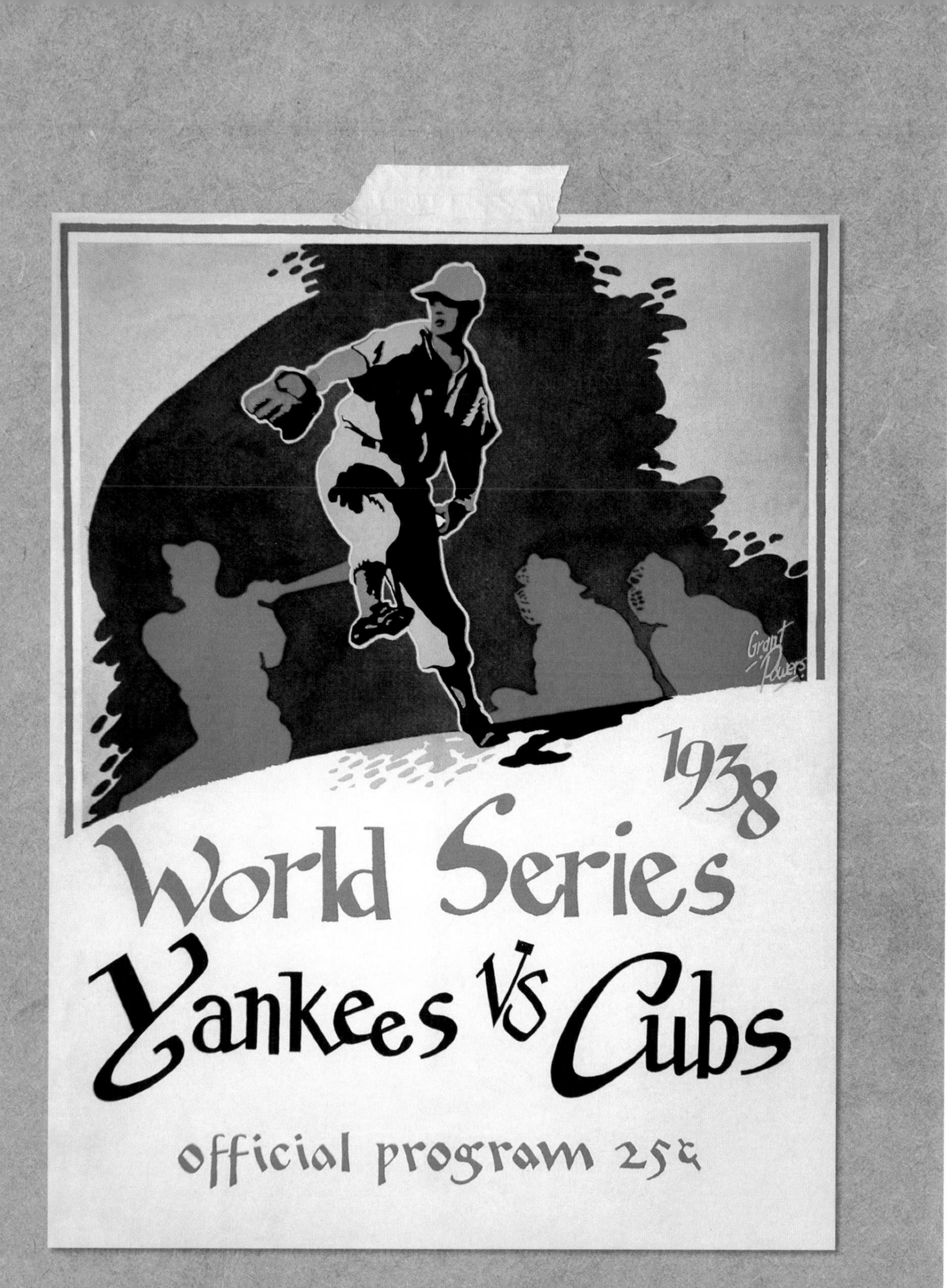

LEFT With the memorable 1938 Series, the New York Yankees became the first team to win three straight world championships by sweeping the Chicago Cubs in four straight games. It was the Yankees' fourth sweep in their last six Series appearances.

With wife Eleanor, 1937

ROLL OF HONOR
Lou Gehrig

Gehrig, getting ready to bat in his 2,000th consecutive game played on May 31, 1938

"Lou didn't need tributes from anyone. His life and the way he lived were tribute enough; he just went out and did his job every day." —BILL DICKEY, teammate, speaking at Gehrig's funeral

Two months after his record 2,130-consecutive-game streak ended, Lou Gehrig delivered his famed farewell address on Lou Gehrig Appreciation Day at Yankee Stadium. He said simply:

"Fans, for the past two weeks you have been reading about the bad break I got. Yet today I consider myself the luckiest man on the face of this earth. I have been in ballparks for seventeen years and have never received anything but kindness and encouragement from you fans.

"Look at these grand men. Which of you wouldn't consider it the highlight of his career just to associate with them for even one day? Sure, I'm lucky. Who wouldn't consider it an honor to have known Jacob Ruppert? Also, the builder of baseball's greatest empire, Ed Barrow? To have spent six years with that wonderful little fellow, Miller Huggins? Then to have spent the next nine years with that outstanding leader, that smart student of psychology, the best manager in baseball today, Joe McCarthy? Sure, I'm lucky.

"When the New York Giants, a team you would give your right arm to beat, and vice versa, sends you a gift—that's something. When everybody down to the groundskeepers and those boys in white coats remember you with trophies—that's something. When you have a wonderful mother-in-law who takes sides with you in squabbles with her own daughter—that's something. When you have a father and a mother who work all their lives so you can have an education and build your body—it's a blessing. When you have a wife who has been a tower of strength and shown more courage than you dreamed existed—that's the finest I know.

"So I close in saying that I may have had a tough break, but I have an awful lot to live for."

When Gehrig finished speaking, Ruth threw his arms around the big first baseman in an impulsive show of affection that brought tears to many eyes in the Stadium that day.

Poster advertising the historic event →

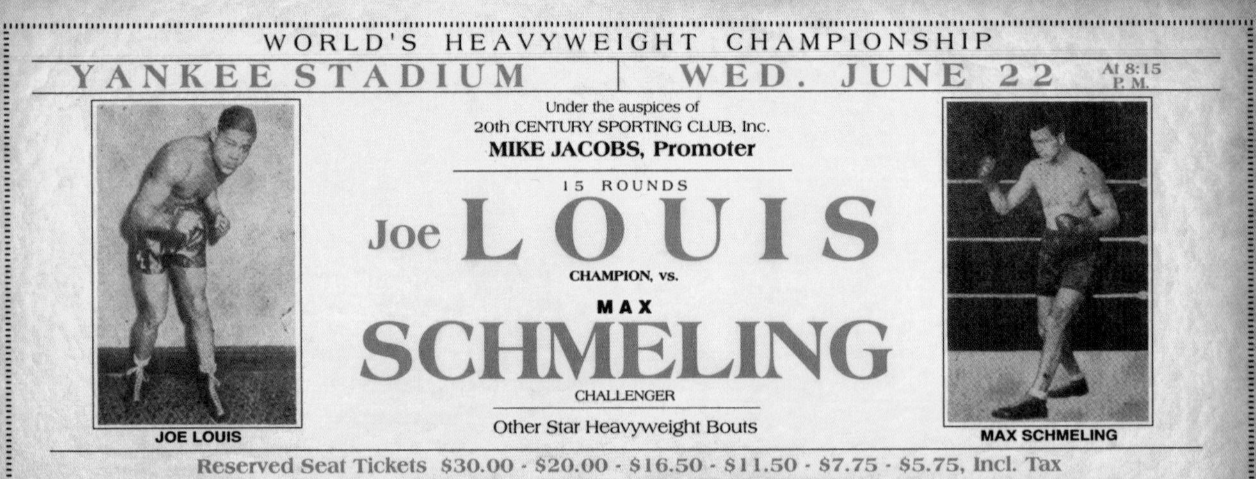

LEFT AND RIGHT In the most politically charged sporting event of all time, Joe Louis knocks down Germany's Nazi poster boy Max Schmeling three times in the first round at Yankee Stadium on June 22, 1938. After the third knockdown, Schmeling's trainer literally threw in the towel.

JOE LOUIS

INNING

3

the 1940s

World War II takes over America—and the Stadium—during the first half of the decade. A parade of Yankees stars changes into uniforms supplied by Uncle Sam. Enough of them remain, however, to win two titles during the war. After V-E Day, the ballclub enjoys two DiMaggio-led V-Y Days—ultimate victory for the Yankees.

"There is always some kid who may be seeing me for the first or last time, (so) I owe him my best." —JOE DIMAGGIO

Young fans admire the façade, 1948

"You saw him standing out there and you knew you had a pretty darn good chance to win the baseball game."
—RED RUFFING, Yankee Hall of Fame pitcher, describing the comfort of seeing DiMaggio in center field

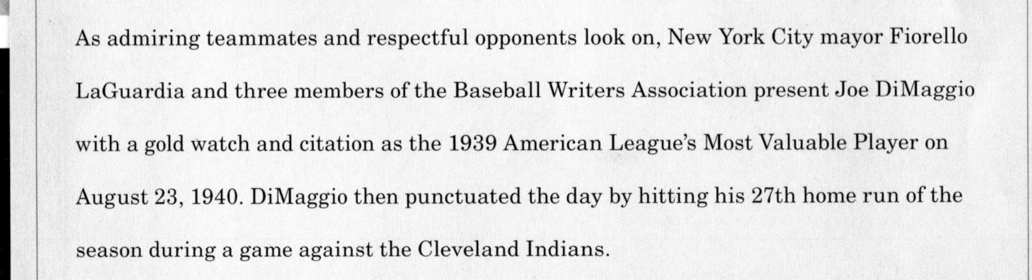
As admiring teammates and respectful opponents look on, New York City mayor Fiorello LaGuardia and three members of the Baseball Writers Association present Joe DiMaggio with a gold watch and citation as the 1939 American League's Most Valuable Player on August 23, 1940. DiMaggio then punctuated the day by hitting his 27th home run of the season during a game against the Cleveland Indians.

LEFT This 1941 Yankees scorecard depicts Hall of Fame catcher Bill Dickey, who caught more than 100 games in thirteen consecutive seasons from 1929 to 1941, an American League record.

BELOW Ted Williams (center) poses with the DiMaggio brothers, Joe and Dom, before a game at Yankee Stadium in 1941. Williams became the last player to hit .400 for a season, but Joltin' Joe hit in a record 56 consecutive games and was the league's Most Valuable Player.

JOE DIMAGGIO'S 56-GAME HITTING STREAK

With this swing, Joe DiMaggio extended his hitting streak to 44 games against the Boston Red Sox at Yankee Stadium on July 1, 1941. He would not be stopped for another twelve games. The nation was captivated by the hitting streak. A song called "Joltin' Joe DiMaggio," composed by Ben Homer with lyrics by Alan Courtney and performed by Les Brown and his Orchestra with Betty Bonney on vocals, hit No. 12 on the pop charts.

"If you said to God, 'Create someone who was what a baseball player should be,' God would have created Joe DiMaggio . . . and he did." —TOM LASORDA, Hall of Fame manager

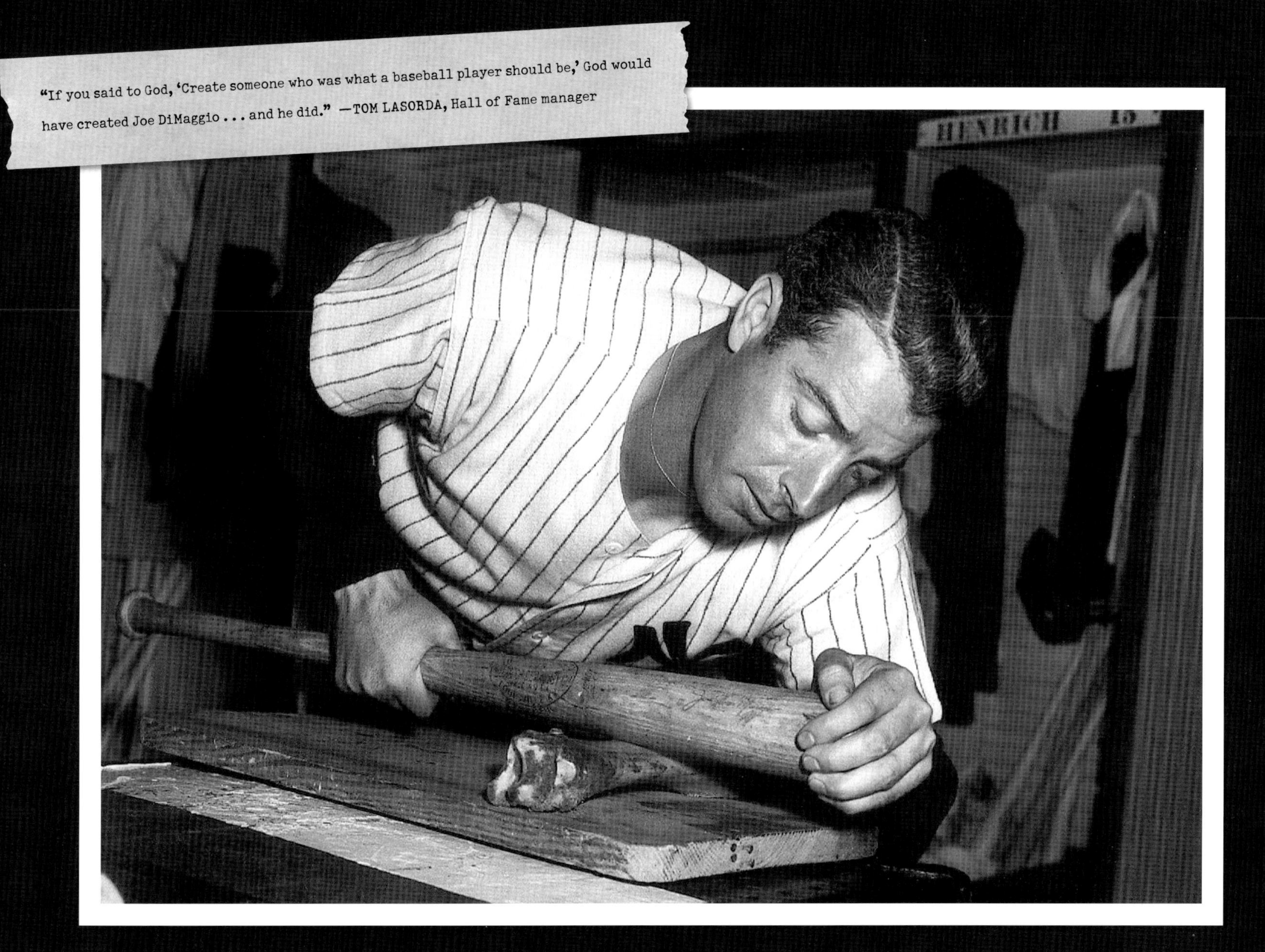

DiMaggio "bones" his bat to strengthen it before a game.

1944 Official Program and Score Card

LEFT By 1943 the Yankees' roster, along with that of most teams, was depleted by the military effort. The Yankees sagged to third place in 1944, and the next year the Ruppert estate sold the franchise to Dan Topping, Del Webb, and Larry MacPhail for $2.8 million. MacPhail introduced New York to night baseball by installing lights atop Yankee Stadium for the 1946 season. Nearly fifty thousand fans attending the first night game at Yankee Stadium on May 28, 1946, saw the home team lose, 2-1, to the Washington Senators. But they ate ballpark hot dogs for dinner!

ABOVE The Yankee Stadium scoreboard and right-center field bleachers in June 1946, shortly after the first night game was ever played.

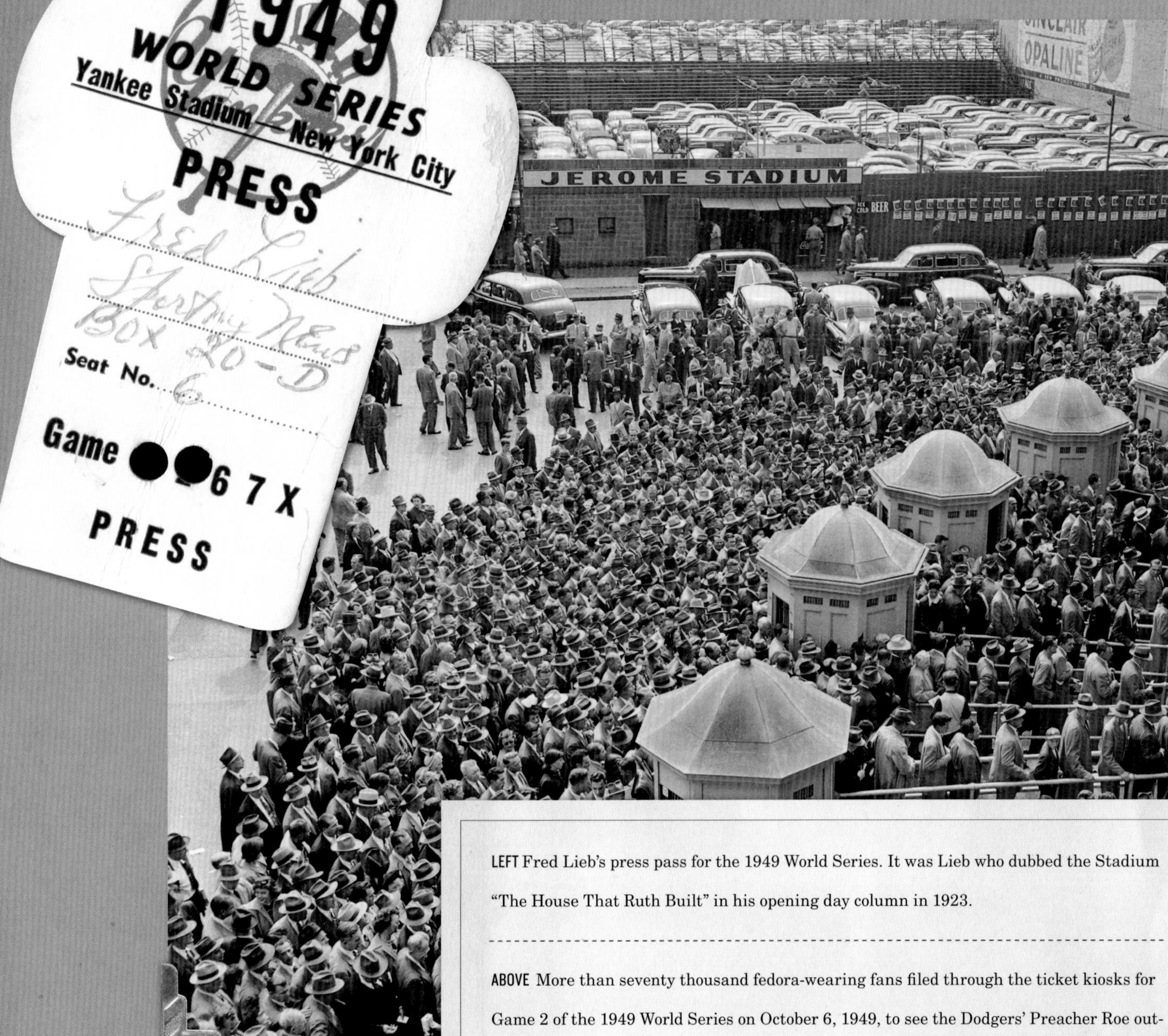

LEFT Fred Lieb's press pass for the 1949 World Series. It was Lieb who dubbed the Stadium "The House That Ruth Built" in his opening day column in 1923.

ABOVE More than seventy thousand fedora-wearing fans filed through the ticket kiosks for Game 2 of the 1949 World Series on October 6, 1949, to see the Dodgers' Preacher Roe out-duel Vic Raschi, 1-0. The Yankees would go on to win the Series in five games, beginning a major league record streak of five consecutive world titles from 1949 to 1953. No other team besides the 1936–39 Yankees has won more than four straight to this day.

ROLL OF HONOR

Joe DiMaggio

Joe DiMaggio takes batting practice at Yankee Stadium in June 1949.

DiMaggio missed half of the season because of a heel injury and pneumonia. When fans welcomed him back on Joe DiMaggio Day on October 1, the Yankee Clipper apologized to the people in the bleachers because the microphones at home plate made him turn his back to them. In his speech he said: "I want to thank the Good Lord for making me a Yankee."

Army's Arnold Tucker (No. 17) returns the opening kickoff against Notre Dame before seventy-four thousand at Yankee Stadium on November 9, 1946. Army, the defending national champion, undefeated in twenty-five games and second-ranked Notre Dame without a loss this season, played to an historic 0-0 tie. The Irish's Johnny Lujack made a brilliant tackle of the Cadet's Doc Blanchard to keep the game scoreless, and Notre Dame would finish No. 1 in the Associated Press poll.

Welterweight champion Sugar Ray Robinson (right) connects with a wicked right against Kid Gavilan of Cuba on his way to a ten-round decision at Yankee Stadium, on September 24, 1948.

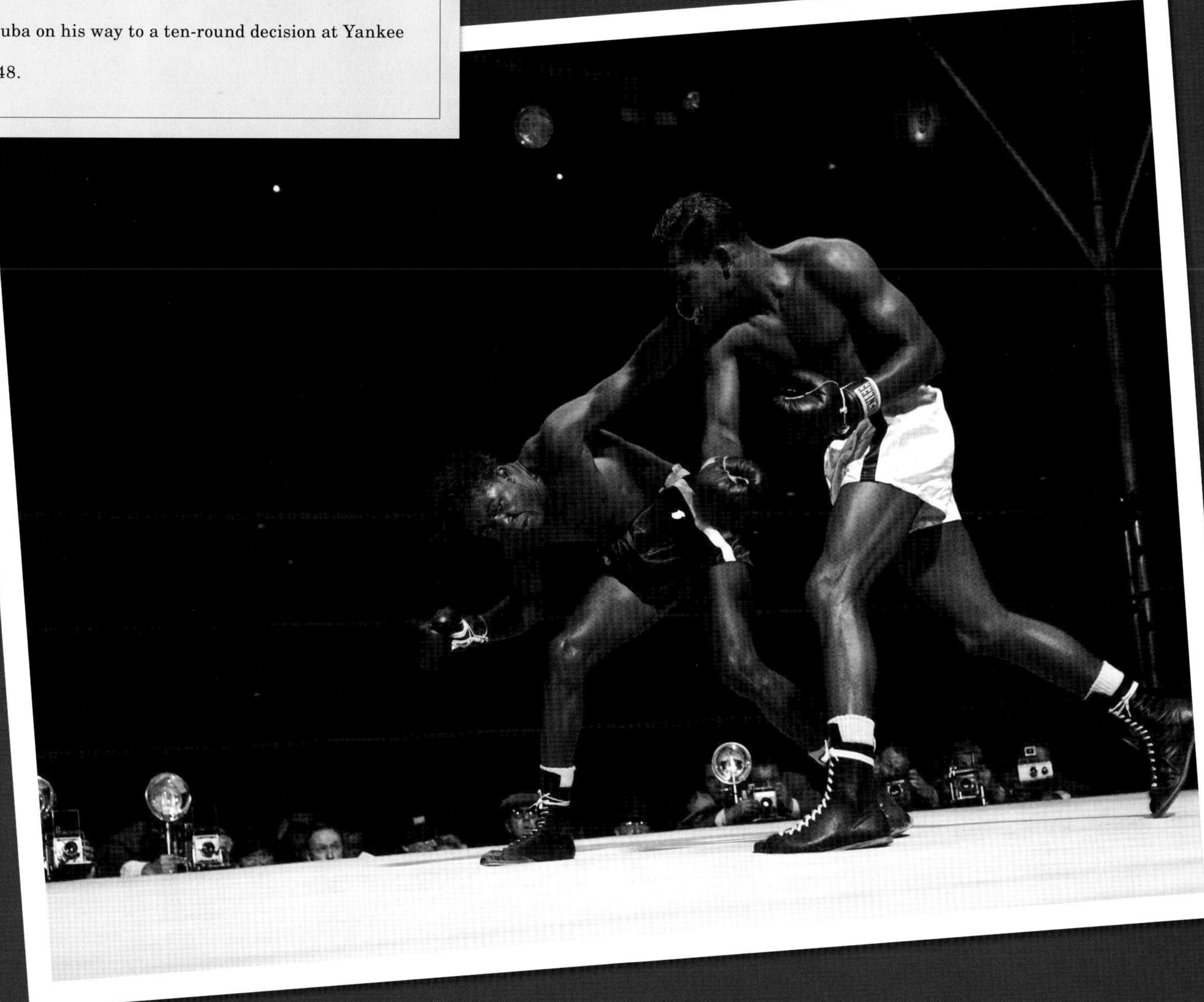

New York City is the epicenter of baseball during the 1950s, and even with Willie and the Duke, Mickey's Yankee Stadium is the best place to be. The Stadium hosts eight World Series and the Yanks win an incredible six, paced by heroes like Mantle, Berra, Ford, and Rizzuto. By the end of the decade, however, the Yankees were the last team standing in Gotham.

"There was a great, dark mystery about (Yankee Stadium) when I first came here from Oklahoma. I still get goose pimples walking inside it. Now I think this is about the prettiest ball park I ever saw." —MICKEY MANTLE

Yankee Stadium façade, circa 1950

George Weiss, Yankees general manager, oversees workers making the final preparations for Opening Day in 1950. The Yankees would unveil their new $100,000 scoreboard, which measures 73 feet long, 34 feet high, and utilizes over 5,000 incandescent lamps.

Legendary catcher Yogi Berra tags out the sliding Philadelphia Phillies shortstop Granny Hamner for an out at home plate to complete a double play in the fourth inning of the Yankees' 5-2 victory in Game 4 of the 1950 World Series. The victory secured the Yankees' 13th championship in twenty-seven years.

"I liked playing in Yankee Stadium. It's a great ballpark . . . . Now it's got a big tradition of twenty-six world championships. My gosh, nobody else has ever done that!" —YOGI BERRA

The Yankees celebrate their third straight championship in 1951. Joe DiMaggio played his last game in the 1951 Series, closing out a legendary career on a winning note, driving in five runs as the Yankees beat the New York Giants in six games. In Joe's thirteen seasons, the Yanks won nine World Series. He finished with a lifetime batting average of .325 and what amounted to automatic election five years later to the Hall of Fame.

DiMaggio, the Yankees center fielder since 1936 and perhaps the most graceful player ever to play the game, after announcing his retirement at age thirty-seven in 1952. "When baseball is no longer fun, it's no longer a game," he said, "and so, I've played my last game of ball."

Yankees catcher Yogi Berra, incredulous that umpire Bill Summers gave the safe sign after Jackie Robinson stole home in the eighth inning of the 1955 Series opener. Berra still insists Robinson was out.

Mel Allen was the voice of the Yankees from 1939 to 1964. His catchphrase "How about that?" and trademark home run call of "Going, going, gone!" became a rallying cry for two generations of fans.

ROLL OF HONOR
Mickey Mantle

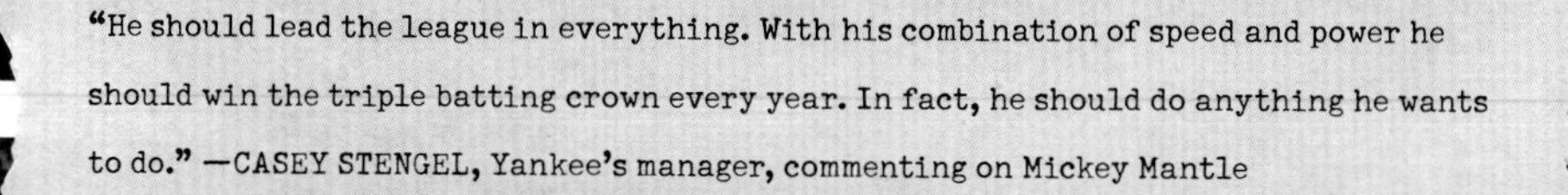
"He should lead the league in everything. With his combination of speed and power he should win the triple batting crown every year. In fact, he should do anything he wants to do." —CASEY STENGEL, Yankee's manager, commenting on Mickey Mantle

Mickey Mantle takes a mighty swing at Yankee Stadium in 1956. That season, the Mick became the only switch-hitter to win the Triple Crown, hitting .353, with 52 home runs and 130 runs batted in. He was named the American League's Most Valuable Player.

1957 World Series Official Program

Mickey Mantle hitting snowballs at Yankee Stadium in February 1957. Mantle had another stellar season that year, winning his second consecutive Most Valuable Player award.

DON LARSEN'S PERFECT GAME

LEFT As second baseman Billy Martin and a string of zeros look on, Don Larsen hurls the final pitch of the only perfect World Series game ever thrown.

OPPOSITE When Brooklyn Dodgers pinch hitter Dale Mitchell strikes out to end Game 5 at Yankee Stadium, catcher Yogi Berra joyfully leaps into Larsen's arms.

"My most special memory is the perfect game that Don Larsen pitched. It never happened before, and it still hasn't happened since. The game lasted only two hours and fifteen minutes. When it was over with, I jumped in his arms. It was just a reaction. It was great. I jumped on him for the heck of it, and then I went off to the clubhouse, and let him get all the glory." —YOGI BERRA

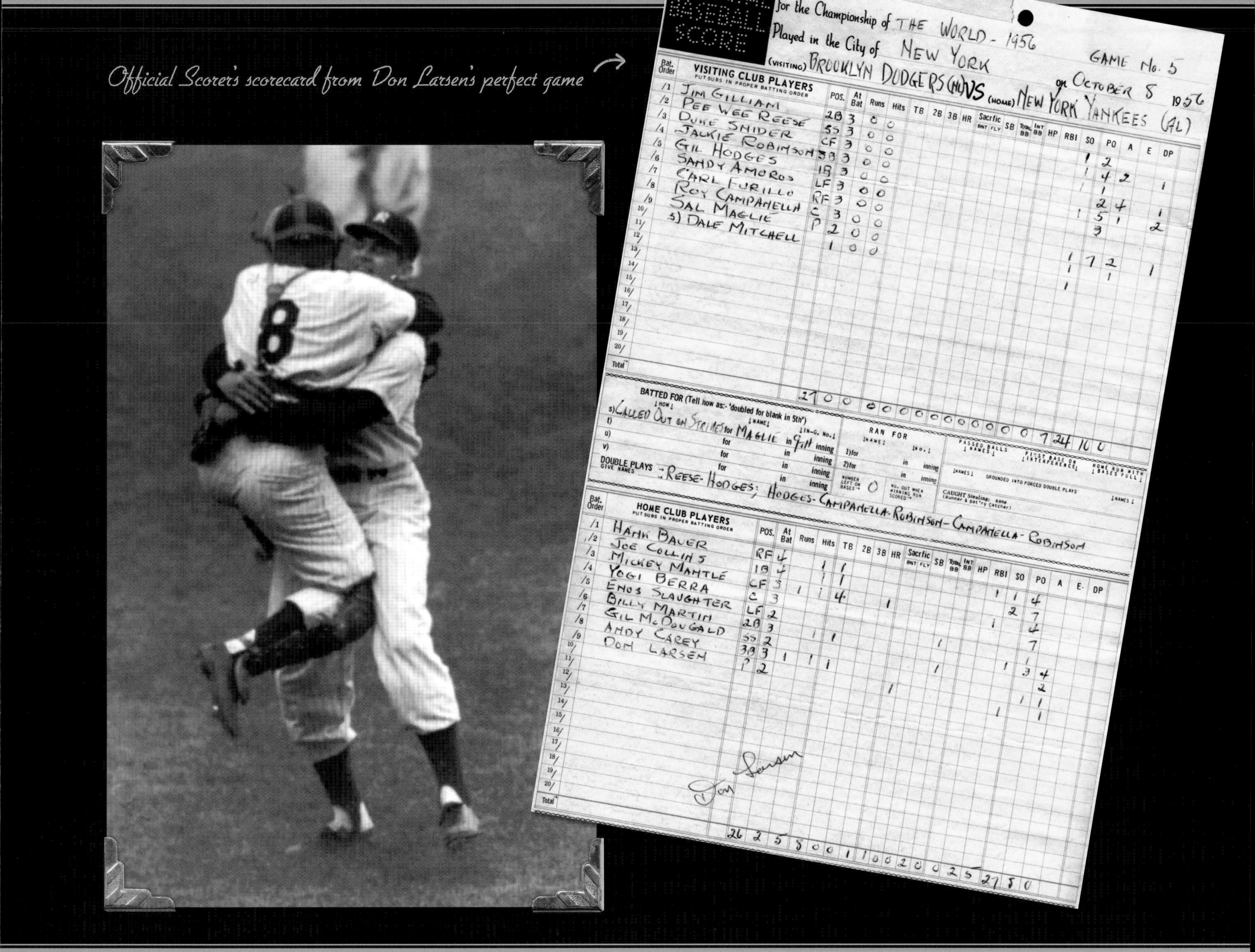

BASEBALL SCORE for the Championship of THE WORLD - 1956
Played in the City of NEW YORK GAME No. 5
(VISITING) BROOKLYN DODGERS (NL) VS (HOME) NEW YORK YANKEES (AL) on OCTOBER 8 1956

Bat. Order	VISITING CLUB PLAYERS	POS.	At Bat	Runs	Hits
1	JIM GILLIAM	2B	3	0	0
2	PEE WEE REESE	SS	3	0	0
3	DUKE SNIDER	CF	3	0	0
4	JACKIE ROBINSON	3B	3	0	0
5	GIL HODGES	1B	3	0	0
6	SANDY AMOROS	LF	3	0	0
7	CARL FURILLO	RF	3	0	0
8	ROY CAMPANELLA	C	3	0	0
9	SAL MAGLIE	P	2	0	0
	s) DALE MITCHELL		1	0	0
Total			27	0	0

BATTED FOR (Tell how as:- 'doubled for blank in 5th')
s) CALLED OUT ON STRIKES for MAGLIE in 9th inning

DOUBLE PLAYS GIVE NAMES: REESE-HODGES; HODGES-CAMPANELLA-ROBINSON-CAMPANELLA-ROBINSON

NUMBER LEFT ON BASES: 0

Bat. Order	HOME CLUB PLAYERS	POS.	At Bat	Runs	Hits	TB
1	HANK BAUER	RF	4		1	1
2	JOE COLLINS	1B	4		1	1
3	MICKEY MANTLE	CF	3	1	1	4
4	YOGI BERRA	C	3			
5	ENOS SLAUGHTER	LF	2			
6	BILLY MARTIN	2B	3		1	1
7	GIL McDOUGALD	SS	2			
8	ANDY CAREY	3B	3	1	1	1
9	DON LARSEN	P	2			
Total			26	2	5	5

Don Larsen

Official Scorer's scorecard from Don Larsen's perfect game

Rocky Marciano beats Archie Moore in the last bout of his boxing career in front of more than sixty-one thousand fans at Yankee Stadium on September 21, 1955. Moore went down for the count in the ninth round. Marciano retired the following year and remains the only heavyweight champion to retire undefeated.

LEFT New York Giants football star Frank Gifford and the team's offensive coordinator Vince Lombardi watch the action from the muddy sidelines of Yankee Stadium during a game in 1956. Three years later, Lombardi would become the head coach of the Green Bay Packers.

BELOW Johnny Unitas (No. 19) leads the Baltimore Colts to victory in sudden-death overtime against the New York Giants, 23-17, in the 1958 NFL Championship Game at Yankee Stadium on December 28, 1958. This title game was the first overtime game in league history and came to be called the "Greatest Game Ever Played."

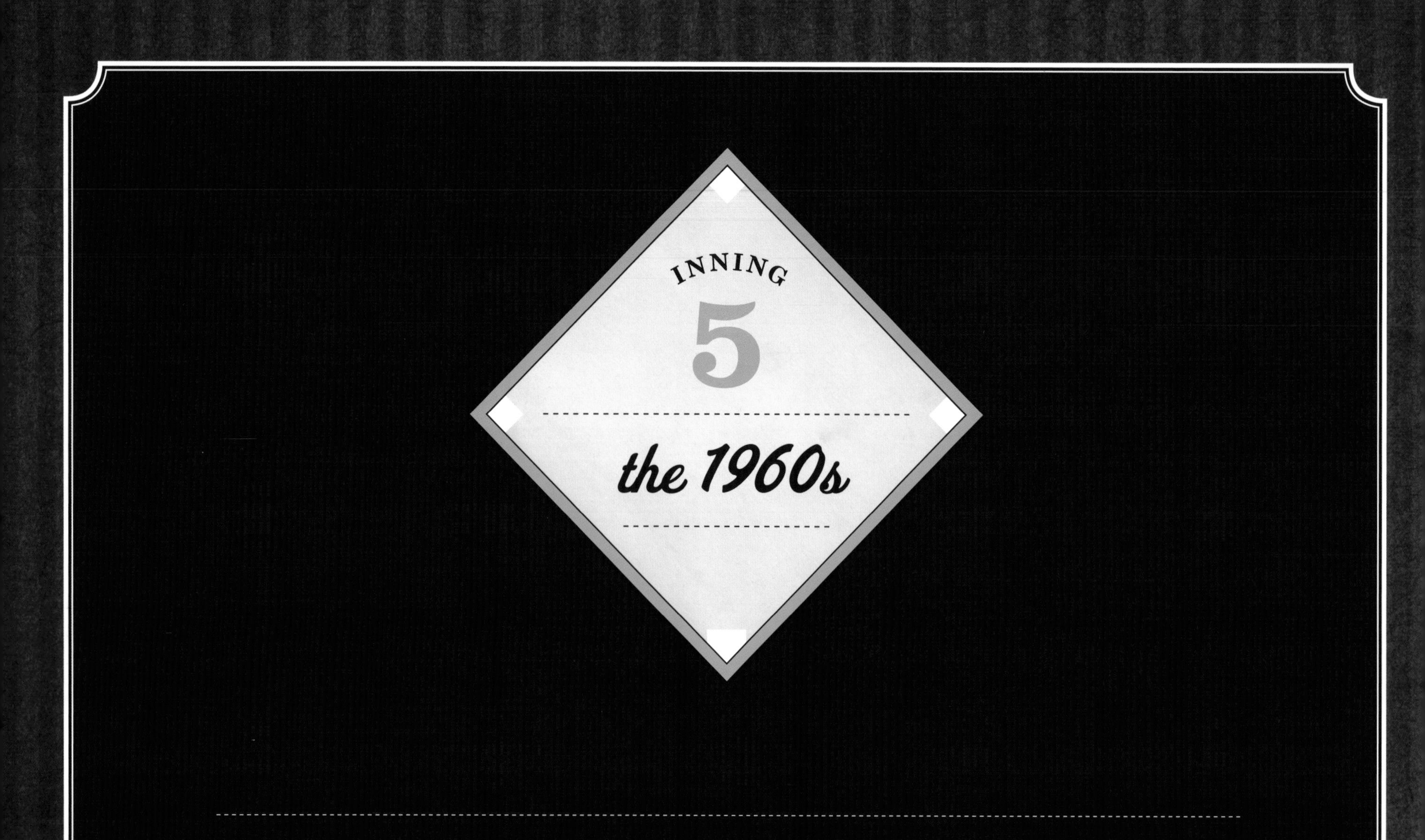

A good start . . . a quiet end. The 1960s roiled the country and sent the Yankees into a tailspin. Even Yogi Berra as manager wasn't enough (though he did win a pennant). Roger Maris kicked things off with his stunning march to 61 homers, but by the end of the 1960s, the Yankees were a second-division regular.

"When I pitched in Yankee Stadium in the World Series, it felt the same as it did every other game, including the games I pitched in the minor leagues there . . . . There was always a big crowd at Yankee Stadium, so pitching in the Series felt no different from any other game." —WHITEY FORD

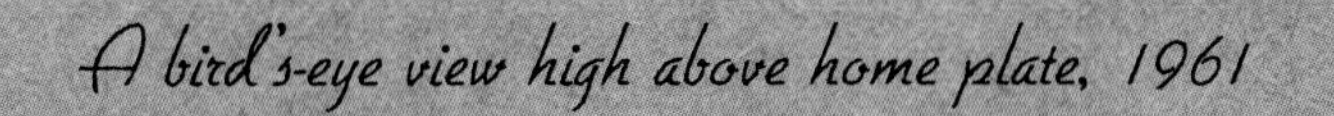

A bird's-eye view high above home plate, 1961

1960 All-Star Game program. Yankee Stadium hosted baseball's All-Star Game for a second time on July 13, 1960. The National League beat the American League 6-0. Whitey Ford was the losing pitcher. Four Yankees, Yogi Berra (catcher), Mickey Mantle (outfield), Roger Maris (outfield), and Bill Skowron (first base) were in the starting lineup; Jim Coates (pitcher) and Elston Howard (catcher) were reserves.

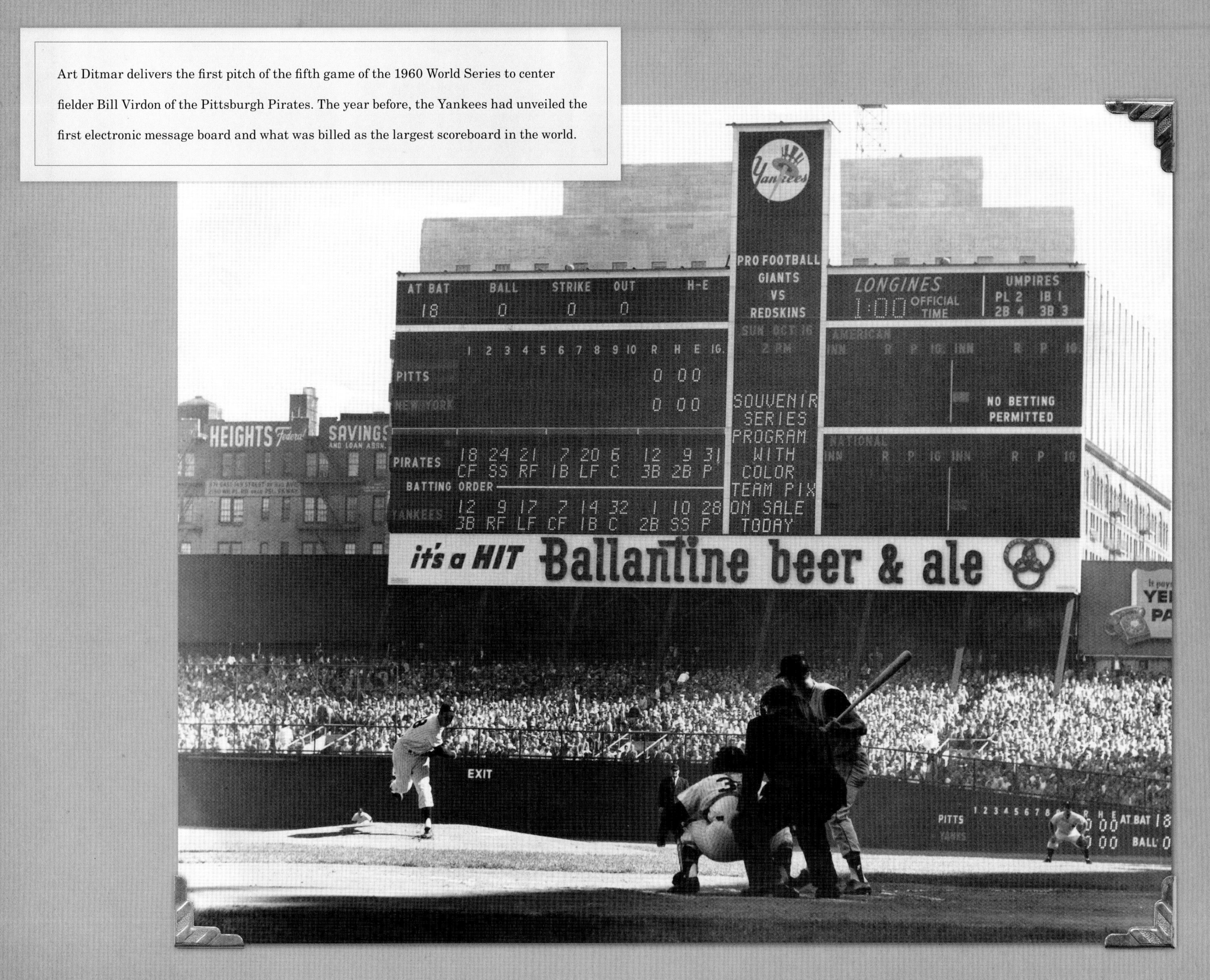

Art Ditmar delivers the first pitch of the fifth game of the 1960 World Series to center fielder Bill Virdon of the Pittsburgh Pirates. The year before, the Yankees had unveiled the first electronic message board and what was billed as the largest scoreboard in the world.

Left-handed pitcher Whitey Ford set a World Series record of 33 consecutive scoreless innings, breaking Babe Ruth's 1916 and '18 record of 29 innings with the Boston Red Sox, when he went 5 shutout innings against the Cincinnati Reds in Game 4 of the 1961 World Series. The Yankees won 7-0 and took the Series in five games.

Whitey Ford pitches to the Dodgers' Frank Howard in the 1963 World Series. Ford holds the Series records for victories, 10, and innings pitched, 146.

"If the World Series was on the line and I could pick one pitcher to pitch the game, I'd choose Whitey Ford every time." —MICKEY MANTLE

The 1963 Official Program and Scorecard

Elston Howard, the first African American player in Yankees history, receives the 1963 American League's Most Valuable Player award from league president Joe Cronin. A two-time Gold Glove catcher, Howard was a member of A.L. pennant-winning Yankees teams in nine of his first ten seasons. Also a respected clubhouse leader, Howard retired in 1968 and became a Yankees coach until his death in 1980.

A "Welcome Yogi" Day pin. Yogi Berra took over as manager in 1964 and led the Yankees to another pennant.

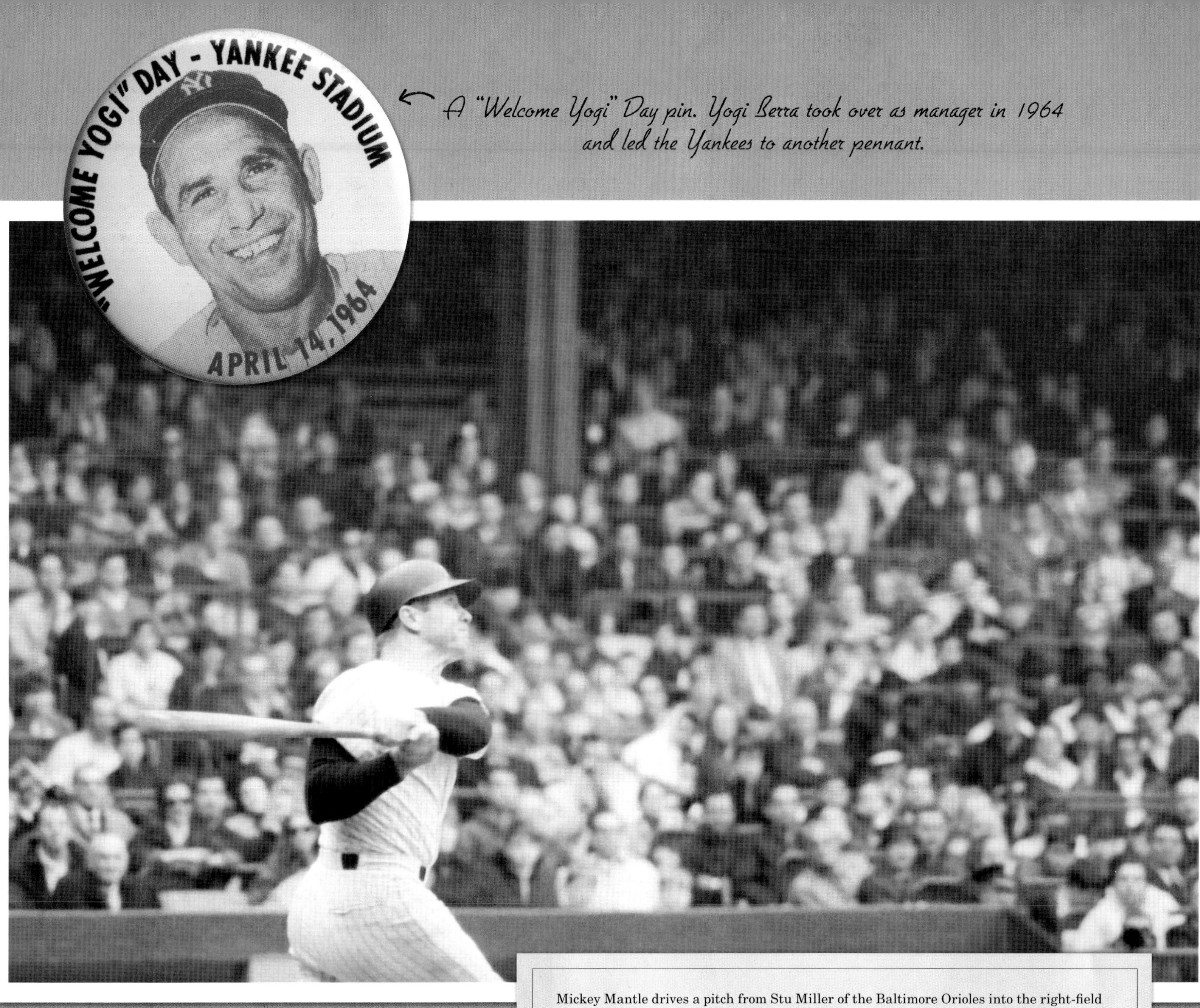

Mickey Mantle drives a pitch from Stu Miller of the Baltimore Orioles into the right-field stands at Yankee Stadium on May 14, 1967, becoming the sixth player in major league history to hit 500 home runs. Mantle finished his career after the 1968 season with 536 career homers. He was 13th on the all-time list after 2007.

RIGHT Mickey Mantle in the Yankee Stadium clubhouse on June 8, 1969. The team celebrated Mickey Mantle Day by retiring his No. 7 in an emotional on-field ceremony. "Playing eighteen years in Yankee Stadium is the best thing that could ever happen to a ballplayer," The Mick tells the crowd.

OPPOSITE A starstruck fan rushes out of the stands to say hello and farewell. More than sixty-one thousand fans showered their retiring hero with a ten-minute standing ovation.

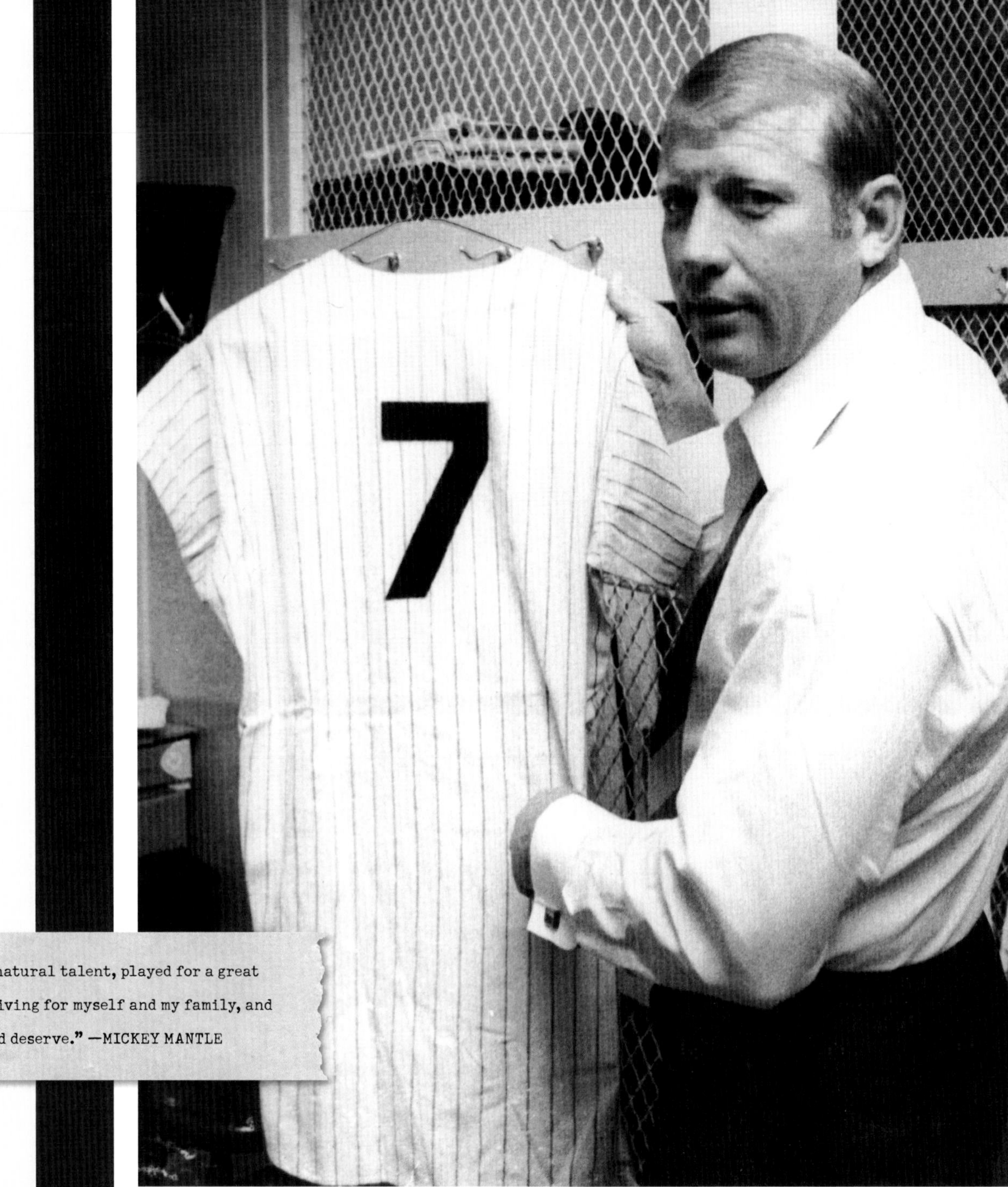

"I have had a great life. I was blessed with more natural talent, played for a great team, with great teammates, made a comfortable living for myself and my family, and acquired more fans and friends than anyone could deserve." —MICKEY MANTLE

MM·7
NEW YORK

In what was called the "Sermon on the Mound," Pope Paul VI celebrates Mass at Yankee Stadium before a crowd of over eighty thousand people on October 4, 1965, during the first-ever papal trip to North America.

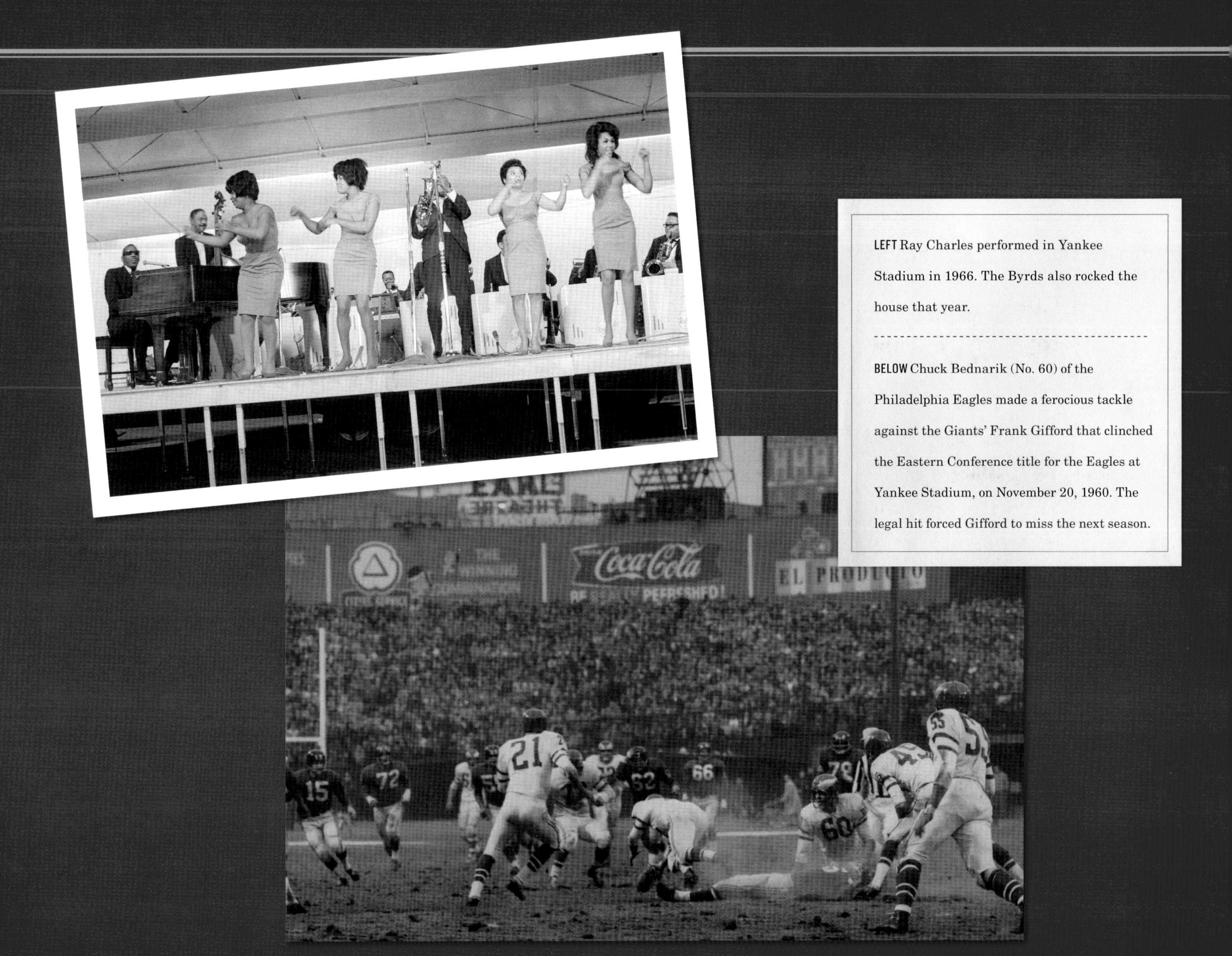

LEFT Ray Charles performed in Yankee Stadium in 1966. The Byrds also rocked the house that year.

BELOW Chuck Bednarik (No. 60) of the Philadelphia Eagles made a ferocious tackle against the Giants' Frank Gifford that clinched the Eastern Conference title for the Eagles at Yankee Stadium, on November 20, 1960. The legal hit forced Gifford to miss the next season.

INNING 6

the 1970s

This roller coaster of a decade includes the coming (and temporary going) of The Boss, the mid-decade renovation of the venerable Stadium, Reggie, the "straw that stirs the drink," and a return—twice!—to World Series glory. Somewhere, the Babe was smiling.

"There's no old and new stadium. To me and my friends, there's only one Yankee Stadium." —WHITEY FORD

A newly retrofitted Yankee Stadium, 1976

RIGHT The Stadium was the star on its 50th anniversary at Old Timers' Day in 1973. Pictured on that day's program from left are managers Miller Huggins, Joe McCarthy, Casey Stengel, and Ralph Houk.

BELOW At a press conference, Michael Burke (left) and George Steinbrenner announce their acquisition of the Yankees from CBS in January 1973. George said, "We plan absentee ownership as far as running the Yankees is concerned. We're not going to pretend we're something we aren't. I'll stick to building ships."

27TH ANNUAL New York Yankees

OLD TIMERS' DAY

Celebrating the 50TH Anniversary of Yankee Stadium...
with representatives of 50 Yankee teams.

LEFT Ron Blomberg rounding the bases at Yankee Stadium against the Red Sox. On Opening Day at Fenway Park in 1973, Blomberg became the first D.H. to appear in the major leagues, drawing a walk with the bases loaded. He remembers, "When I got to first base, I looked at the umpire and I didn't know what to do. He told me to just do what I always do. [After the game,] what seemed like a hundred reporters were asking me questions about being the first D.H. There aren't too many firsts in baseball, and I'm a first . . . . Who ever thought that one at-bat could be so important? It's incredible. I was an answer in Trivial Pursuit. I was a question in *Jeopardy*."

BELOW Jim ("Catfish") Hunter wearing his Yankees cap for the first time in January 1975. He won twenty-three games for the Bombers in 1975 and was a World Series starter in each of the next three seasons. Arm trouble ended his career at age thirty-three, but he still went to Cooperstown. His plaque reads: "The bigger the game, the better he pitched."

RIGHT Phil Rizzuto, the former Yankees shortstop-turned-broadcaster, surveys the construction that was transforming Yankee Stadium in December 1974. "I was sick when they dug the first hunk of dirt out of the infield," said "the Scooter." "I have spent half my life in this stadium." Ten new rows of seats were added to the upper deck, and the steel columns supporting the second and third decks were removed in the renovation. Workers replaced the old wooden seats with wider, plastic ones and erected a replica of the famed Stadium façade atop a 560-foot-long scoreboard that would stretch across the rear of the center-field bleachers. The state-of-the-art board had the first "Telescreen" to show fans instant replays of the action. The renovated park accommodates only fifty-four thousand fans, but nearly every seat is a good one.

Roy White played left field for the Yankees from 1965 to 1979, spanning the reconstruction of the Stadium:

"The old Yankee Stadium left field was notorious for the sun. From three o'clock on in the afternoon the sun was straight, dead-on in the left fielder's eyes. There was no home field advantage for anybody with that sun. October is always the worst, especially if there's a crystal-clear bright sky. Most of the time, I just hoped it would be overcast. Knowing the history of Yankee Stadium's left field, you didn't want to lose a ball in the sun out there, and that was always in the back of your mind . . . . it was terrifying.

"I never lost a ball in the sun in the old Stadium. When Yankee Stadium was renovated I lost a ball once. Ron Guidry was pitching against the Texas Rangers in 1978. Al Oliver was the batter, and he sliced one to left. I had to run to my right, and the ball kept slicing, and it was right into the sun, and there was no way out of it. That ball ended up hitting me on the left arm for a two-base error, and a runner scored. It didn't cost us the game—maybe it cost Guidry a shutout—but I think we won 4-1 or 5-1.

"It's ironic that the only time I lost a ball in the sun was in the new Stadium. When they renovated Yankee Stadium, the sun's angle wasn't quite as bad because they moved home plate back maybe twenty or thirty feet. It had to be much later in the day before the sun had its full effect. In the new stadium, you can get through seven innings without having the sun get really bad."

YANKS AT SHEA
PHONE 592 8200

The remodeled Yankee Stadium opened on April 15, 1976, with the National Anthem and an 11-4 rout of the Minnesota Twins. Mickey Rivers, Chris Chambliss, and Oscar Gamble each knocked in two runs for the home team. Like in 1923, the Yankees opened their new stadium in grand style by reaching the World Series, though it would be another year before they captured the championship trophy.

22 642E 15
SEC. BOX SEAT

UPPER BOX
Est. Price $7.41
City & St. Tax .59
$8.00
ADMIT ONE
GAME 5
Yankee Stadium

AMERICAN REVOLUTION BICENTENNIAL
AMERICAN LEAGUE CHAMPIONSHIP SERIES
EAST vs. WEST
1776-1976

Yankees

Yankee Stadium
NEW YORK CITY

GAME 5
RAIN CHECK subject to the conditions set forth on back hereof.
DO NOT DETACH THIS COUPON
LELAND S. McPHAIL, JR.
President American League

"It was absolutely thrilling because normally the people at Yankee Stadium are well-behaved and they don't run on the field en masse. Once in a while a kook will run on the field. Thousands of people ran onto the field and I did nothing to stop them. I never said a word. I couldn't; the Marines could not have stopped them. They just engulfed the field." —BOB SHEPPARD, public-address announcer

ABOVE On October 14, 1976, Chris Chambliss hits Mark Littell's first pitch in the last of the ninth inning for a home run at Yankee Stadium, giving New York a 7-6 victory over the Kansas City Royals in the decisive Game 5 of the American League Championship Series. The blast sent the Bombers to their first World Series since 1964 and triggered a mad rush of joyous fans pouring onto the field to mob their new hero as he circled the bases.

1976 American League Championship Series ticket to Game 5 at Yankee Stadium

ROLL OF HONOR

Reggie Jackson

Reggie Jackson blasts his record 3rd consecutive home run in the sixth and final game of the World Series at Yankee Stadium, on October 18, 1977. Jackson cracked his three home runs off three straight pitches from three different pitchers, joining Babe Ruth as the only man to homer three times in a World Series game. But "Mr. October" is the only slugger to hit five homers in a single series.

"The fans were chanting, 'Reg-gie! Reg-gie! Reg-gie!' (as) I was rounding first, and (Dodgers first baseman) Steve Garvey winked at me, and at third base, Ron Cey touched his hat. It was almost like I was running on air." —REGGIE JACKSON

ABOVE Reggie celebrates the 1977 championship with manager Billy Martin (left). Reggie had said, “I’m the straw that stirs the drink,” and indeed he was for the Yankees’ championship teams of 1977 and ’78.

BELOW Writers who covered the 1977 World Series were given this pin, which allowed them into the locker room and onto the field to interview players.

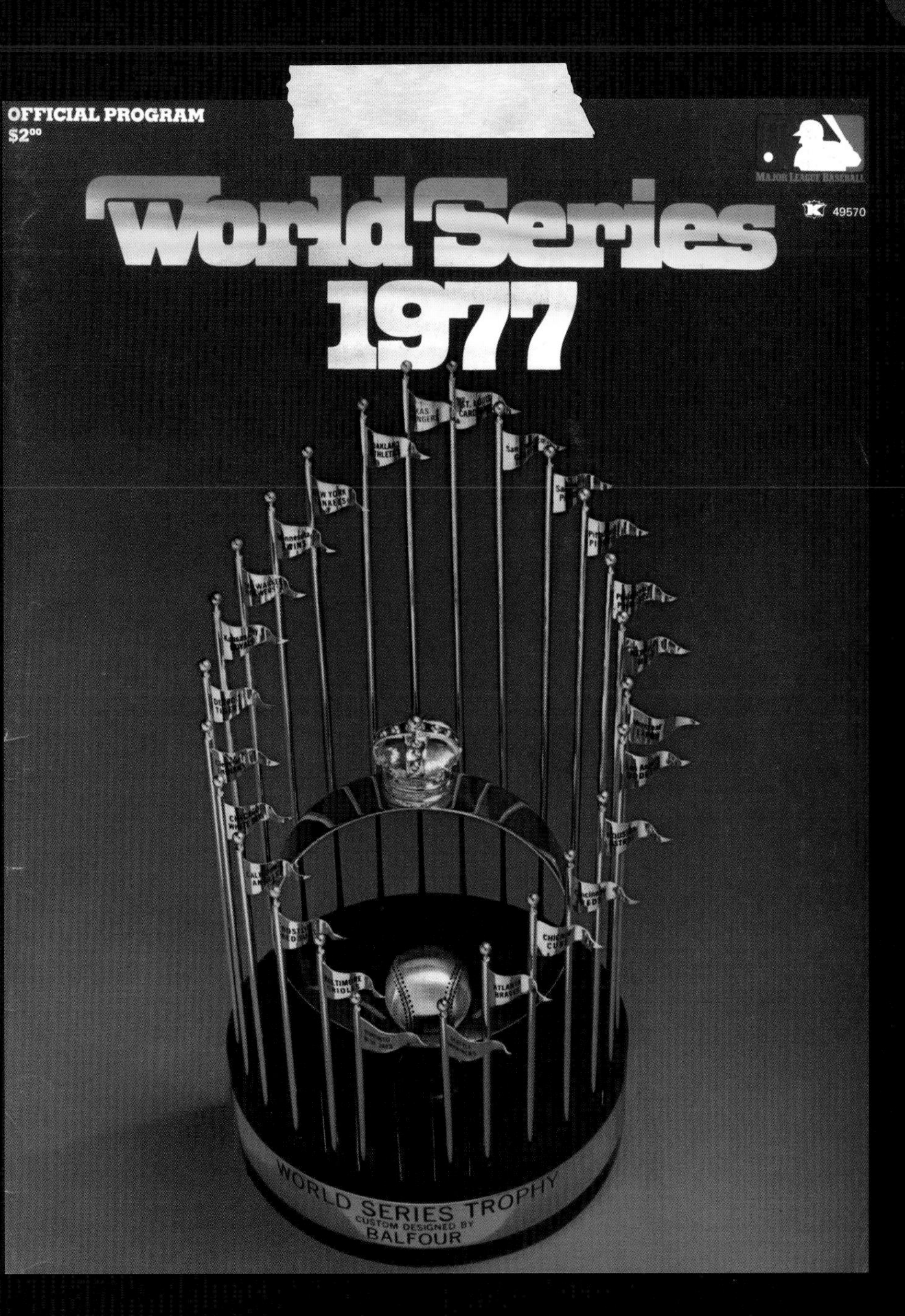

1977 World Series Official Program

Ron Guidry soaks his left arm and munches on a spare rib after establishing a franchise record by striking out 18 batters in the Yankees' 4-0 win over the California Angels at Yankee Stadium on June 16, 1978. That year was Guidry's peak, with Louisiana Lightning's 25-3 record and 1.74 earned run average rating among the best seasons any pitcher has ever had.

LEFT Thurman Munson, the 1970 American League's Rookie of the Year and Most Valuable Player of 1976, hit for a .292 average over eleven seasons and was at his best in the clutch, batting .373 over three World Series.

ABOVE Munson was a leader on three pennant winners and two World Series championship teams, and was also the first Yankee captain since Lou Gehrig four decades before. He tragically died at age thirty-two when the jet plane he was piloting crashed near the Canton, Ohio, airport on August 2, 1979, when he was headed to his nearby home for a visit with his wife and children. Munson's uniform, No. 15, was retired, and he was honored with a plaque in Monument Park. Outfielder Bobby Murcer accompanies wife Diana Munson at Thurman's commemorative ceremony in Yankee Stadium, September 20, 1980.

Pelé, the World Cup soccer star from Brazil and the sport's most famous player, joined the New York Cosmos in 1976, bringing international exposure to the North American Soccer League. Here he puts the moves on a Washington Diplomats defender during the Cosmos' 2-0 victory at Yankee Stadium on August 17, 1976.

ABOVE Ken Norton (right) playfully chases Muhammad Ali, the world heavyweight champion, in a game of tag across the Yankee Stadium outfield during a publicity session for their title fight, on September 28, 1976. Ali successfully defended his title with a hard-fought, fifteen-round unanimous decision. It was the thirtieth and last championship bout contested at Yankee Stadium.

RIGHT With the Yankees out of the World Series for the first time in three years, Yankee Stadium played host to an event of worldwide significance when Pope John Paul II celebrated Mass on October 2, 1979.

INNING 7

the 1980s

For the first time since they started playing the World Series, a decade went by without the Yankees holding up the trophy. Pennantless fans still got to fall in love with Donnie Baseball, Louisiana Lightning, Sweet Lou, Winfield, and others, while also enjoying the soap opera of revolving Yankee managers. Never a dull moment with The Boss in his Stadium office!

"I can still remember walking out of the locker room, going down the tunnel and back up that ramp, then coming up the stairs into the dugout and seeing the stadium unfold in front of my eyes for the first time. At most ballparks you walk into the dugouts and everything is flat, in a sense. But in Yankee Stadium, there's so much of the stadium above you as you come out from the dugout. It's like the stands are growing up above you." —DAVE RIGHETTI, pitcher

Yankee Stadium and the surrounding area, 1988

RIGHT Bob Lemon, who skippered the Yankees to a world title in 1978, returned as manager for a second time in September 1981, replacing Gene Michael. His low-key approach helped the Yankees reach the Series again, but it was their last high point for more than a decade.

OPPOSITE The fielding wizardry of third baseman Graig Nettles foiled several Dodgers' rallies in the 1981 World Series — conjuring images of his sparkling '78 Series form — but the Yankees stumbled, losing in six games. A colorful member of a team nicknamed "The Bronx Zoo," Nettles once said: "When I was a little boy, I wanted to be a baseball player and join a circus. With the Yankees I've accomplished both."

Billy Martin returns to Yankee Stadium for his third stint as manager in 1983. Martin was hired and fired by owner George Steinbrenner five times, the last time in 1988, a year before his death in an automobile accident on Christmas Day.

Good seats were at a premium that day.

On July 4, 1983 at Yankee Stadium, Dave Righetti pitches the first no-hitter for the Yankees since Don Larsen's perfect game in the 1956 World Series. "It wasn't a full house that day, but the Yankees were playing the Red Sox . . . and it was hot," the pitcher remembers. Despite the heat, Righetti struck out Wade Boggs, who would retire with 3,010 lifetime hits, for the final out of a 4-0 shutout.

Righetti recalls: "Going out for the ninth inning the fans were cheering long before I hit the mound, so I was definitely thinking about it when I was warming up. It actually gave me a little bit of a boost because I was fatiguing in my legs. But I was gonna give it everything I had. The one thing I regret is that I never got to go into the clubhouse with my teammates. The press grabbed me on the field to take pictures and I was interviewed in the dugout for television, so I never got to go inside and soak it in with my teammates."

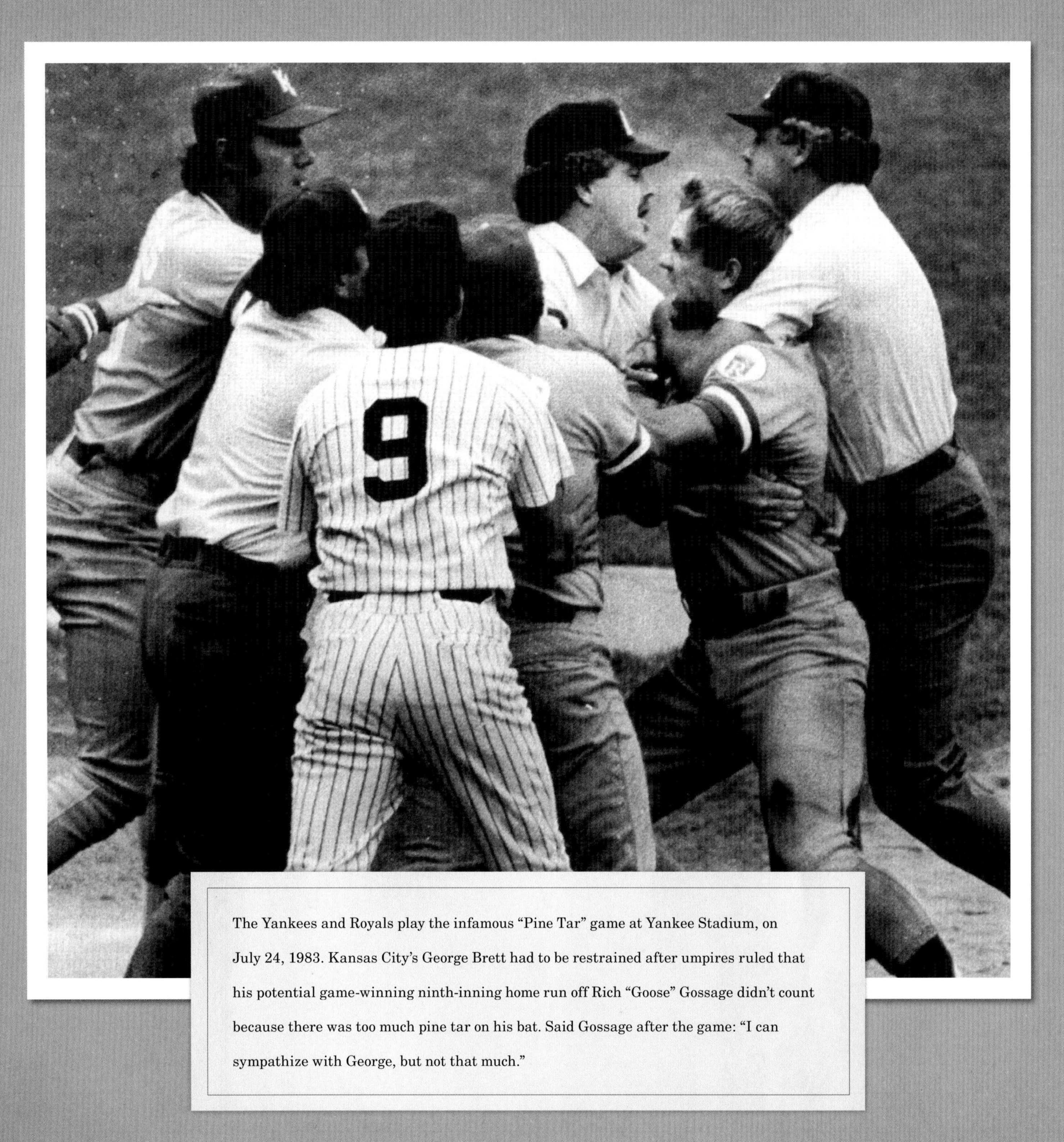

The Yankees and Royals play the infamous "Pine Tar" game at Yankee Stadium, on July 24, 1983. Kansas City's George Brett had to be restrained after umpires ruled that his potential game-winning ninth-inning home run off Rich "Goose" Gossage didn't count because there was too much pine tar on his bat. Said Gossage after the game: "I can sympathize with George, but not that much."

Dave Winfield, who was drafted to play professional basketball, football, and baseball, was one of the best athletes to wear pinstripes. Winfield knocked in 100 runs six times, and he batted .340 in 1984, narrowly losing the league's batting title to teammate Don Mattingly.

ABOVE Willie Randolph scores a run against the Baltimore Orioles at Yankee Stadium in 1983. He played more games at second base (1,688) than any other player in Yankees' history. Willie joined the Yankees in 1976, and in his first six seasons, the Bombers won five divisional titles, four American League pennants, and two World Series titles.

RIGHT Ricky Henderson, the Yankees all-time stolen bases leader, set the single-season franchise mark with 93 steals in 1988.

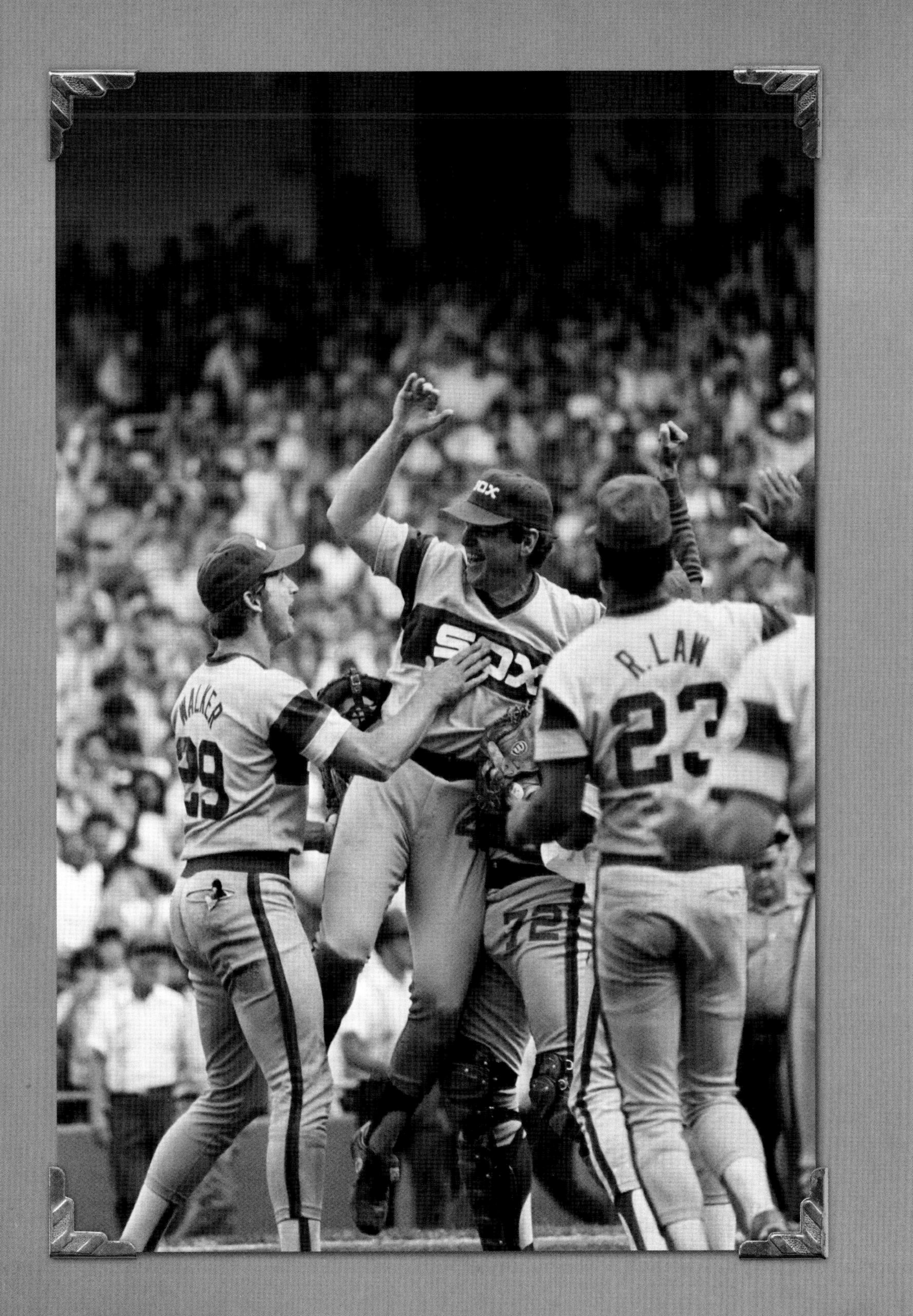

August 4, 1985. On a day in which 54,032 fans honor their favorite shortstop and broadcaster with Phil Rizzuto Day, Chicago's Tom Seaver records his 300th victory at Yankee Stadium. Seaver became only the seventeenth pitcher in major league history to reach 300 wins—and the first ever to achieve the feat at Yankee Stadium. "It was like I was levitating on the mound," said Seaver afterward.

ROLL OF HONOR

Don Mattingly

Don Mattingly won the American League batting title with a .343 average in 1984, and the next season, he won the league's Most Valuable Player award. In 1987, Mattingly hit ten home runs during an eight-game stretch, tying a major league record by going deep in eight consecutive games. Mattingly was only the tenth player in the Yankees storied history to be named as team captain.

First baseman Don Mattingly was a slick fielder, winning 9 Gold Glove awards for fielding excellence. A back injury six years into his career, along with playing on poor teams, robbed "Donnie Baseball" of the chance to join Yankee greats with World Series championships. His only playoff games were in 1995, when the Yanks lost to Seattle.

The Beach Boys played the Stadium on June 26, 1988. From left: Al Jardine, Mike Love, and Carl Wilson.

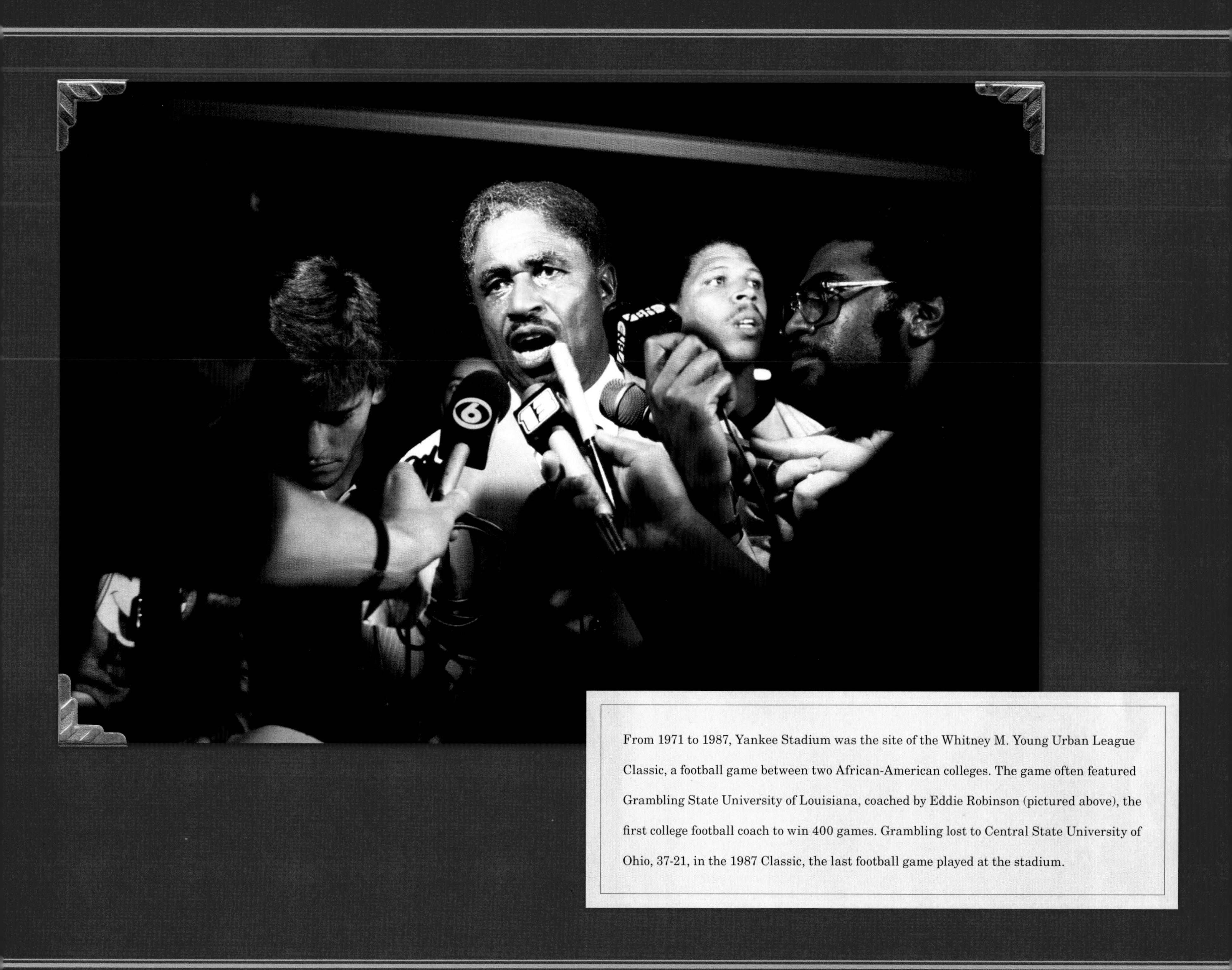

From 1971 to 1987, Yankee Stadium was the site of the Whitney M. Young Urban League Classic, a football game between two African-American colleges. The game often featured Grambling State University of Louisiana, coached by Eddie Robinson (pictured above), the first college football coach to win 400 games. Grambling lost to Central State University of Ohio, 37-21, in the 1987 Classic, the last football game played at the stadium.

INNING

8

the 1990s

In the tradition of Huggins and McCarthy, a new Yankees leader emerged. Joe Torre, a quiet leader, began a playoff-appearance streak that would stretch into the new millennium. Meanwhile, in the footsteps of Ruth, DiMaggio, and Mantle came Derek Jeter, Bernie Williams, Paul O'Neill, and others. And on the mound behind Ford and Rags strode Mariano Rivera. A core of Yankee greats led the team to three World Series titles and put the Yankees once more atop the baseball world.

"When I was with the Mets and we played the Mayor's Trophy Game in Yankee Stadium, I never played. But I always thought about what it would be like pitching in Yankee Stadium because of all the tradition that goes along with being a Yankee and playing in that ballpark." —DWIGHT GOODEN, pitcher

Yankee Stadium and surrounding area, 1993

RIGHT In the most amazing feat ever performed by a physically challenged athlete in professional sports, Jim Abbott of the Yankees, who was born without a right hand, pitched a 4-0 no-hitter against the visiting Cleveland Indians, on September 4, 1993. After getting Carlos Baerga to ground out to shortstop Randy Velarde for the final out, Abbott opened his arms wide and blared, "How about that, baby!"

BELOW Jim Leyritz celebrates after hitting a dramatic home run in the fifteenth inning to defeat the Seattle Mariners in Game 2 of the 1995 division series. He also changed the tide of the 1996 World Series in Game 4 with an eighth-inning homer off Atlanta's Mark Wohlers. Of his 13 career postseason hits, eight cleared the fences.

With his father scheduled for open-heart surgery the next day, thirty-one-year-old Dwight Gooden, the former Mets phenom who was considered washed-up, revived the magic of his early Mets years in just his seventh start for the Yankees by pitching his only no-hitter, 2-0, against the Seattle Mariners on May 14, 1996. After Paul Sorrento popped out to Derek Jeter for the final out, "Dr. K" hugged catcher Joe Girardi.

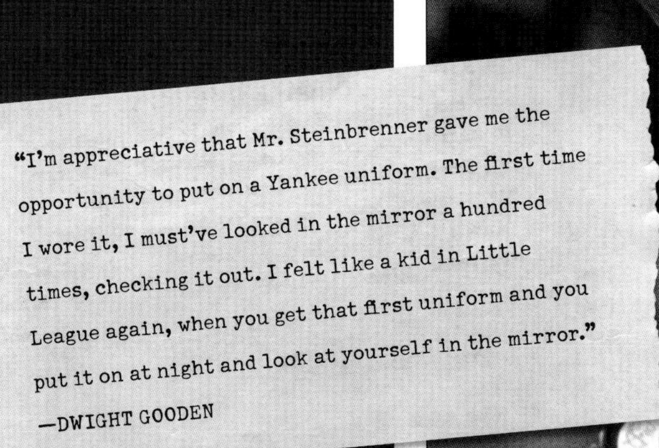

"I'm appreciative that Mr. Steinbrenner gave me the opportunity to put on a Yankee uniform. The first time I wore it, I must've looked in the mirror a hundred times, checking it out. I felt like a kid in Little League again, when you get that first uniform and you put it on at night and look at yourself in the mirror."

—DWIGHT GOODEN

ROLL OF HONOR

Derek Jeter

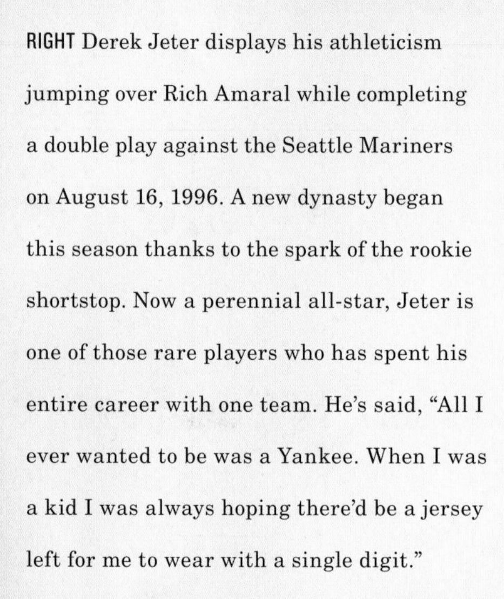

RIGHT Derek Jeter displays his athleticism jumping over Rich Amaral while completing a double play against the Seattle Mariners on August 16, 1996. A new dynasty began this season thanks to the spark of the rookie shortstop. Now a perennial all-star, Jeter is one of those rare players who has spent his entire career with one team. He's said, "All I ever wanted to be was a Yankee. When I was a kid I was always hoping there'd be a jersey left for me to wear with a single digit."

The Yankees were trailing the Orioles, 4-3, in Game 1 of the 1996 American League Championship Series. In the bottom of the eighth inning, Derek Jeter hit a fly ball to the right-field wall that Baltimore's Tony Tarasco seemed about to catch, but twelve-year-old fan Jeffrey Maier reached over with his mitt and deflected the ball. It was ruled a home run, and the Yankees went on to win the game, the series, and the world title.

The Yankees beat Atlanta 3-2 in Game 6 of the 1996 World Series for their first title in eighteen years. Third baseman Wade Boggs celebrated by trotting around Yankee Stadium on a policeman's horse. After nine All-Star seasons with the hated Boston Red Sox, Boggs signed a free-agent contract with the Yankees in December 1992. He played for the Yanks from 1993 to 1997. However, his memories of Yankee Stadium begin far before it was his home field. It was at Yankee Stadium in 1986 while playing for the Red Sox that Boggs learned of his mother's death.

"Before I signed with the Yankees [in 1992], I sat down with my father and discussed the situation that I'd have to deal with. I'd be here eighty-one days of the season, at a place where I got a tragic phone call. The memories are still vivid, but at least those memories were all on the visitors' side. I just dissolved myself from the fact that the phone ever rang. I brought in all new memories when I came to the home side."

BELOW David Wells, the burly pitcher who once wore an actual Babe Ruth cap during a game, enters Yankee Stadium lore on May 17, 1998. He threw a perfect game against the Minnesota Twins, and was carried off the field by his teammates. Billy Crystal greeted him after the game and quipped: "I got here late. What happened?"

RIGHT This ticket got a lucky fan into Game 2 of the 1998 World Series. Home runs by Bernie Williams and Jorge Posada propelled the Yankees to a 9-3 victory over the San Diego Padres. The Yankees won an amazing 114 games that season and then swept the Padres to win their 24th World Championship.

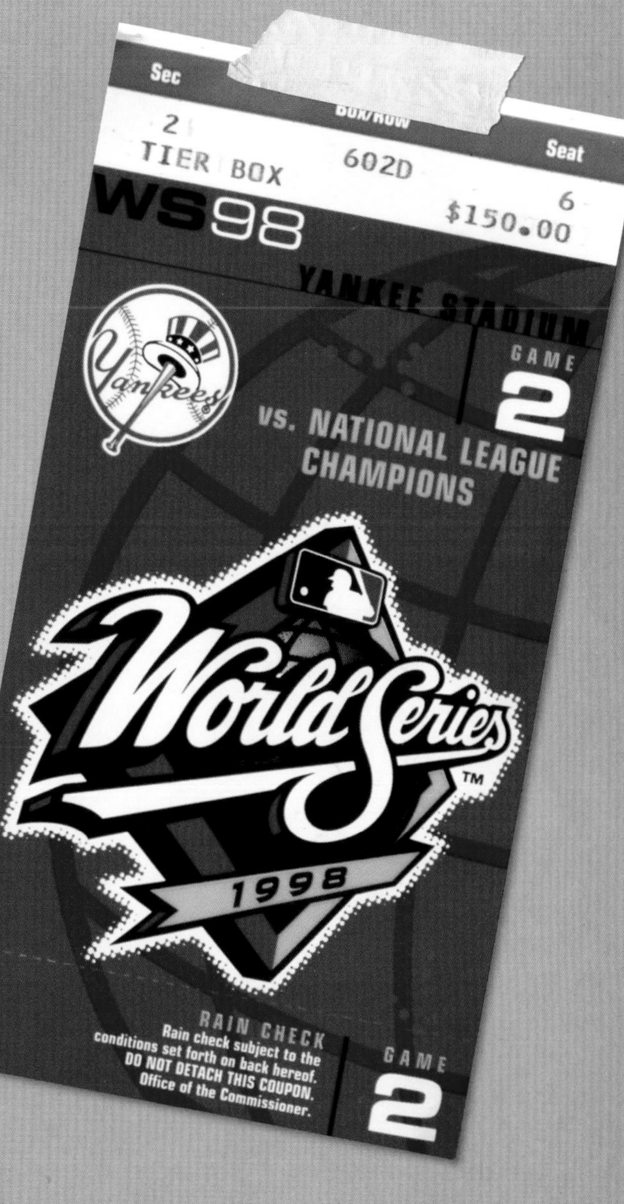

DAVID CONE'S PERFECT GAME

On July 18, 1999, Yogi Berra (left) and Don Larsen attend the game at Yankee Stadium to celebrate Yogi Berra Day. Right-hander David Cone took the mound against the Montreal Expos and pitched a perfect game of his own.

"What an honor. With all the Yankee legends here today, Don Larsen in the park, Yogi Berra Day, it makes you stop and think about the Yankee magic and the mystique of this ballpark." —DAVID CONE, after pitching a perfect game at Yankee Stadium

After recording the final out, a jubilant Cone drops to his knees and hugs catcher Joe Girardi. "My heart was pumping," said Cone afterward. "I could feel it through my uniform."

Derek Jeter smiles for a photo in the tunnel leading to the locker room after the Yankees play baseball's last game of the century and complete a four-game World Series sweep of the Atlanta Braves on October 27, 1999.

This ring honors the Yankees on the occasion of their twenty-fifth World Series title.

More than anyone else, it was Mariano Rivera that propelled the Yankees into World Series champions for three consecutive seasons, as he was on the mound to secure the final out in each of the three clinching games in 1998, 1999, and 2000.

BEYOND THE YANKEES: 1990s

Nearly eighty thousand fans packed Yankee Stadium for a rally celebrating South African freedom fighter Nelson Mandela's prison release and the end of apartheid on June 21, 1990. Mandela put on a New York Yankees baseball jacket and cap and exclaimed, "I am a Yankee!"

LEFT Billy Joel at the piano performing the first rock concert held at Yankee Stadium on June 22, 1990.

ABOVE U2 also performed in the Bronx on their "Zoo TV" tour in 1992. At one point, lead singer Bono told the crowd: "I dreamed I saw Joe DiMaggio, dancing with Marilyn Monroe."

INNING

9

the 2000s

And now . . . the end is near . . . and so we face the final curtain! The beginning of the end of Yankee Stadium I.0 starts with another World Series triumph, continues with the coming of A-Rod, and wraps up with the end of the highly successful Joe Torre era.

"The first time I trotted out to right field at Yankee Stadium, wearing a Yankees uniform, I was already a veteran ballplayer. I'd seen a lot. I'd already won a World Series ring in Cincinnati. I was no kid. And about halfway out there, it occurred to me that this is exactly the spot where Babe Ruth used to play. He used to hit home runs into those bleachers right behind me. That's when I really looked around, and noticed how enormous it all is." —PAUL O'NEILL, right fielder

The sun goes down and the lights come up at Yankee Stadium, 2000.

Roger Clemens of the Yankees fires the barrel of Mike Piazza's broken bat in his direction in Game 2 of the World Series against the Mets on October 22, 2000. The incident aroused heated public debate in light of Clemens's beaning of Piazza in July. Four nights later, the Yankees won the first Subway Series in forty-four years, finishing off the Mets in five games for their 26th championship.

RIGHT On September 25, 2001, a memorial service was held at the Stadium for the victims and heroes of the September 11 terrorist attacks. Families of firefighters and tearful onlookers listen while Bette Midler sings "Wind Beneath My Wings."

BELOW Just weeks after the tragedy, the Yankees helped to uplift the spirit of New York with three straight dramatic World Series victories at the Stadium. They won Game 4 on Derek Jeter's walk-off home run after a two-out, game-tying homer in the ninth by Tino Martinez. They also took Game 5 after a two-out, game-tying homer in the ninth by Scott Brosius.

Tino Martinez exults after Yanks clinch the 2001 American League pennant.

On June 13, 2003, Roger Clemens becomes the third pitcher to strike out 4,000 batters and records his 300th career victory against the St. Louis Cardinals at Yankee Stadium.

Ticket from Roger Clemens's 300th win on June 13, 2003

ABOVE Aaron Boone smacks a walk-off home run in the bottom of the eleventh inning of Game 7 of the 2003 American League Championship Series to beat the Boston Red Sox 6-5 at Yankee Stadium, once again breaking the hearts of Red Sox Nation.

RIGHT Yankees reliever Mariano Rivera tips his cap to the home fans after a 5-4 win at Yankee Stadium on July 16, 2006. By shutting down the visiting Chicago White Sox, Rivera recorded his 400th career save, becoming the first American League closer ever to save 400 games for one team.

ROLL OF HONOR

Alex Rodriguez

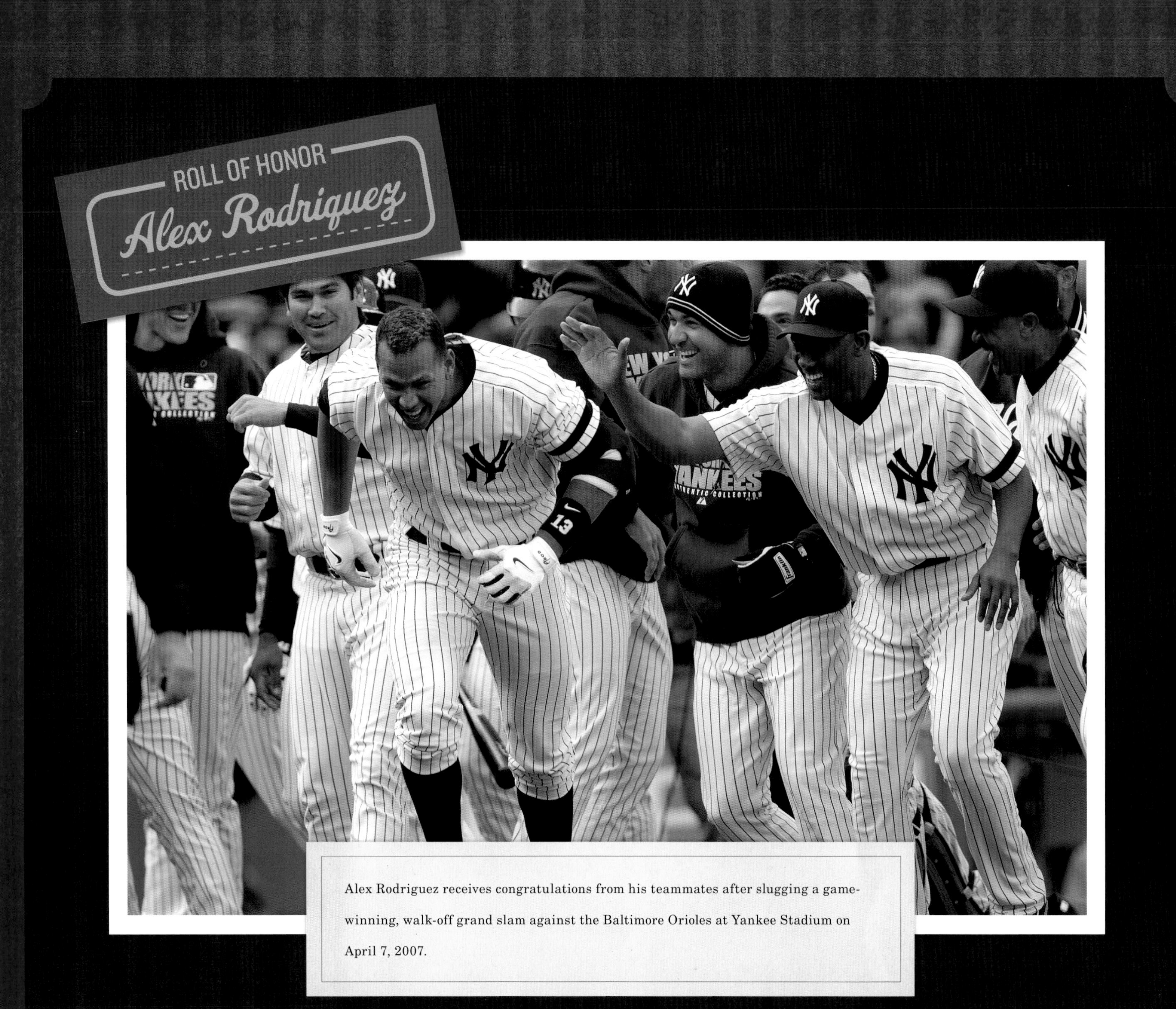

Alex Rodriguez receives congratulations from his teammates after slugging a game-winning, walk-off grand slam against the Baltimore Orioles at Yankee Stadium on April 7, 2007.

"He's one of the best in the game . . . . After he hits his 500th career home run, he's going to make a run at 700 or even 800." —ALBERT PUJOLS, All-Star first baseman of the St. Louis Cardinals, commenting on Alex Rodriguez

Rodriguez circles the bases after he homered into Yankee Stadium's left-field seats off Kansas City's Kyle Davies on August 4, 2007, to become the 22nd player in major league history to reach 500 home runs. At thirty-two years and eight days, he was the youngest to reach the milestone, making him the slugger most likely to be the next challenger to baseball's career home run mark.

RIGHT Yankee Stadium paid homage to its baseball history by creating Monument Park, where the team honors its legends with monuments and plaques in the left-centerfield section of Yankee Stadium. The first monuments in the old Stadium, dedicated to the memories of Lou Gehrig, Miller Huggins, and Babe Ruth, had been in fair territory.

BELOW Visitors to today's Yankee Stadium can admire the row of retired jersey numbers. Starting with Lou Gehrig's No. 4 in 1939, the Yankees have retired fifteen uniform numbers to honor sixteen players and a manager. The jersey numbers, in the order they were retired: 4, Lou Gehrig; 3, Babe Ruth; 5, Joe DiMaggio; 7, Mickey Mantle; 37, Casey Stengel; 8, Bill Dickey; 8, Yogi Berra; 16, Whitey Ford; 15, Thurman Munson; 32, Elston Howard; 9, Roger Maris; 10, Phil Rizzuto; 1, Billy Martin; 44, Reggie Jackson; 23, Don Mattingly; 49, Ron Guidry.

LEFT Public address announcer Bob Sheppard, still the voice of Yankee Stadium since 1951.

BELOW Eddie Layton played "Take Me Out to the Ballgame" during the seventh-inning stretch of every game, until retiring after the 2003 season. Eddie joined the Yankees as organist in 1967.

"I'm aware of the tradition and of the great people who have played there before me. Sometimes I would look around and say, 'Oh, man, this is huge. This is very big.' I felt very lucky to be in a position like that."
—BERNIE WILLIAMS, center fielder

Since 2003, no stadium has welcomed more fans than Yankee Stadium. More than four million Yankees fans have showed up at the ballpark each season since 2004, with 4,243,780 spinning through the turnstiles in 2006, the highest single-season attendance in Yankee Stadium history. Yankee Stadium takes a final bow as host of the All-Star Game in July 2008. Four months later, the wrecking ball comes out and the big ballpark in the Bronx will be torn down, making way for a new stadium that will witness new memories, new legends, and new World Series triumphs.

References

BOOKS

Anderson, Dave, M. Chass, R. Creamer, & H. Rosenthal. *The Yankees: The Four Fabulous Eras of Baseball's Most Famous Team.* New York: Random House, 1979.

Baseball: The Biographical Encyclopedia. Edited by David Pietrusza, Matthew Silverman, and Michael Gershman. New York: Total Sports, 2000.

Gershman, Michael. *Diamonds: The Evolution of the Ballpark.* Boston: Houghton Mifflin Company, 1993.

Hoppel, Joe. *The Series: An Illustrated History of Baseball's Postseason Showcase.* St. Louis: The Sporting News Publishing Company, 1990.

New York Yankees Information & Record Guide. New York Yankees Official Publication, 2000.

One Hundred Years: New York Yankees: The Official Retrospective. New York: Ballantine Books, 2003.

Stout, Glen. *Yankees Century: 100 Years of New York Yankees Baseball.* Boston: Houghton Mifflin Company, 2002.

WEB SITES

www.baseball-almanac.com
www.baseball-reference.com
www.baseballhalloffame.org
http://newyork.yankees.mlb.com

Image Credits

Every effort has been made to trace copyright holders. If any unintended omissions have been made, becker&mayer! would be pleased to add appropriate acknowledgments in future editions.

Cover: (baseball) Sotheby's; (tickets) National Baseball Hall of Fame Library, Cooperstown, NY; (stadium photo) Al Bello/Getty Images

Page 7: Corbis

Page 8: National Baseball Hall of Fame Library MLB Photos via Getty Images (left)

Page 9: Bettmann/Corbis (top); Diamond Images/Getty Images (bottom)

Page 10: Mark Rucker/Transcendental Graphics/Getty Images

Page 11: B. Bennett/Getty Images (top); Bettmann/Corbis (bottom)

Page 12: Bettmann/Corbis

Page 13: National Baseball Hall of Fame Library, Cooperstown, NY

Page 14: Mark Rucker/Transcendental Graphics/Getty Images

Page 15: Sotheby's (left); New York Times Co./Getty Images (right)

Page 16: B. Bennett/Getty Images

Page 17: National Baseball Hall of Fame Library, Cooperstown, NY

Page 18: Underwood & Underwood/Corbis

Page 19: Bettmann/Corbis

Page 21: AP Photo

Page 22: Bettmann/Corbis

Page 23: CBS Photo Archive/Getty Images (top); Bettmann/Corbis (bottom left); National Baseball Hall of Fame Library, Cooperstown, NY (bottom right)

Page 24: Hulton-Deutsch Collection/Corbis (left); Bettmann/Corbis (right)

Page 25: Diamond Images/Getty Images

Page 26: Bettman/Corbis (all)

Page 27: Bettmann/Corbis (top); AP Photo (bottom)

Page 28: AP Photo (bottom)

Page 29: Allsport/Hulton Archive/Getty Images

Page 31: Bettmann/Corbis

Page 32: AP Photo

Page 33: National Baseball Hall of Fame Library, Cooperstown, NY (left); Mark Rucker/ Transcendental Graphics/Getty Images (right)

Page 34: Bettmann/Corbis

Page 35: AP Photo/Preston Stroup

Page 36: National Baseball Hall of Fame Library, Cooperstown, NY (left); Bettmann/Corbis (right)

Page 37: National Baseball Hall of Fame Library, Cooperstown, NY (left); Bettmann/Corbis (right)

Page 38: National Baseball Hall of Fame Library MLB Photos via Getty Images

Page 39: Ralph Morse/Time Life Pictures/Getty Images (top); Bettmann/Corbis (bottom)

Page 40: Bettmann/Corbis

Page 41: Bettmann/Corbis (all)

Page 42: Bettmann/Corbis

Page 43: Bettmann/Corbis

Page 45: Frederic Lewis/Getty Images

Page 46: AP Photo

Page 47: AP Photo

Page 48: Bettmann/Corbis

Page 49: Bettmann/Corbis

Page 50: Grey Villet/Time Life Pictures/Getty Images

Page 51: AP Photo

Page 52: Arnold Newman/Getty Images

Page 53: National Baseball Hall of Fame Library, Cooperstown, NY (left); Bettmann/Corbis (right)

Page 54: Bettmann/Corbis

Page 55: AP Photo (left); National Baseball Hall of Fame Library, Cooperstown, NY (right)

Page 56: Yale Joel/Life Magazine/Time & Life Pictures/Getty Images

Page 57: Robert Riger/Getty Images (all)

Page 59: Bettmann/Corbis

Page 60: Diamond Images/Getty Images

Page 61: Bettmann/Corbis

Page 62: Bettmann/Corbis

Page 63: Robert Riger/Getty Images (top); Blank Archives/Getty Images (bottom)

Page 64: Bettmann/Corbis (left); National Baseball Hall of Fame Library, Cooperstown, NY (right)

Page 65: AP Photo (all)Page 66: Bettmann/Corbis

Page 67: Bettmann/Corbis (bottom)

Page 68: B. Bennett/Getty Images

Page 69: Bettmann/Corbis

Page 70: Bill Eppridge/Time Life Pictures/Getty Images

Page 71: Michael Ochs Archives/Getty Images (top); Kidwiler Collection/Diamond Images/Getty Images (bottom)

Page 73: AP Photo/Marty Lederhandler

Page 74: Olen Collection/Diamond Images/Getty Images (left); National Baseball Hall of Fame Library, Cooperstown, NY (right)

Page 75: Louis Requena/MLB Photos via Getty Images (top); AP Photo/Ray Stubblebine (bottom)

Page 77: AP Photo/Ron Frehm (top); AP Photo/Harry Harris (bottom)

Page 78: Sahm Doherty/Time Life Pictures/Getty Images

Page 79: National Baseball Hall of Fame Library, Cooperstown, NY (left); Bettmann/Corbis (right)

Page 80: Louis Requena/MLB Photos via Getty Images

Page 81: AP Photo (top left); National Baseball Hall of Fame Library, Cooperstown, NY (bottom left and right)Page 82: AP/Wide World Photo

Page 82: AP Photo

Page 83: Diamond Images/Getty Images (left); AP/Wide World Photo (right)

Page 84: George Tiedemann/GT Images/Corbis

Page 85: Bettmann/Corbis (left); Dirck Halstead/Time & Life Pictures/Getty Images (right)

Page 87: Rich Clarkson/Allsport/Getty Images

Page 88: AP Photo/Harry Harris

Page 89: Focus on Sport/Getty Images

Page 90: Olen Collection/Diamond Images/Getty Images

Page 91: Barton Silverman/New York Times Co./Getty Images (top); National Baseball Hall of Fame Library, Cooperstown, NY (bottom)

Page 92: Bruce Bennett Studios/Getty Images

Page 93: Rich Pilling/MLB Photos (all)

Page 94: B. Bennett/Getty Images (top); Bettmann/Corbis (bottom)

Page 95: Bettmann/Corbis

Page 96: Jon Kirn/MLB Photos via Getty Images (left); Michael Zagaris/MLB Photos via Getty Images (right)

Page 97: MLB Photos via Getty Images

Page 98: AP Photo

Page 99: Ronald C. Modra/Sports Imagery/Getty Images

Page 101: AP Photo/Adam Nadel

Page 102: Focus on Sport/Getty Images (top); AP Photo/Louis Requena (bottom)

Page 103: AP Photo/Kevin Larkin

Page 104: AP Photo/Louis Requena

Page 105: AP Photo/Mark Lennihan

Page 106: AP Photo/Ron Frehm

Page 107: AP Photo/Louis Requena (left); National Baseball Hall of Fame Library, Cooperstown, NY (right)

Page 108: AP Photo/Kathy Willens

Page 109: AP Photo/Kathy Willens

Page 110: National Baseball Hall of Fame Library, Cooperstown, NY (left); AP Photo/Mark Lennihan (right)

Page 111: Rob Tringali/Sportschrome/Getty Images

Page 112: Maria Bastone/AFP/Getty Images

Page 113: AP Photo/Ed Bailey (left); Patti Ouderkirk/WireImage/Getty Images (right)

Page 115: Al Martin/MLB Photos via Getty Images

Page 116: Matt Campbell/AFP/Getty Images

Page 117: Reuters/Corbis (top); AP Photo/Kathy Willens (bottom)

Page 118: AP Photo/Lou Rocco (left); National Baseball Hall of Fame Library, Cooperstown, NY (right)

Page 119: David Bergman/Corbis (top); Anthony J Causi/Icon SMI/Corbis (bottom)

Page 120: Tomasso DeRosa/Corbis News Agency/Corbis

Page 121: Justin Lane/epa/Corbis

Page 122: Rich Pilling/MLB Photos (top); Diamond Images/Getty Images (bottom)

Page 123: Reuters/Corbis (top); AP Photo/Asbury Park Press, Jim Connolly (bottom)

Page 124: AP Photo/Richard Drew

back cover: Bettmann/Corbis (top right); National Baseball Hall of Fame Library, Cooperstown, NY (bottom left)

About the Author

A lifelong Yankees fan, David Fischer has authored numerous books on sports, including *Smithsonian Q&A Baseball* (HarperCollins, 2007), *Greatest Sports Rivalries* (Barnes&Noble, 2005), and *Roberto Clemente: Trailblazer of the Modern World* (World Almanac Library, 2004), as well as coauthored *Sports of the Times* (St. Martin's Press, 2003). He has also written for the *New York Times*, *Sports Illustrated For Kids*, and Major League Baseball Publications, worked at the *National Sports Daily* and NBC Sports, and was a contributing writer at *Yankees Magazine* from 1993 to 1997. Fischer currently lives in River Vale, New Jersey.

Acknowledgments

This book would not have been possible without the creativity, sound judgment, and tireless work of my collaborators at becker&mayer! The scope of the book was greatly enhanced by the imagination of editor Meghan Cleary, photo editor Chris Campbell, and designer Kasey Free at becker&mayer! Many thanks to copy editor Dana Henricks and proofreader Avra Romanowitz for making me look good and for keeping me honest. Thanks also to James Buckley Jr. and Brian Arundel for bringing me on board. Naturally, this project would have been difficult to complete without the understanding and support of my wife, Carolyn, and my children, Rachel and Jack. Finally, to Robert L. Fischer, for making me a Yankees fan. Many others contributed ideas, time, advice and encouragement. They include Ian O'Connor, Alan Schwarz, Gregg Mazzola, Tim Wood, and Tom Bannon. To all of them, and to numerous other friends and associates who shared my vision, my deep and abiding thanks.